The Taking
of MH370

Jeff Wise

THE
**YELLOW
CABIN**
PRESS

To Sandra, Rem, and Seb

CONTENTS

PART 1

The Triple-Disappearing Airplane

1.

MARCH 8, 2014

The first 40 minutes, at least, everyone can agree on. At 41 minutes past midnight, the wheels of the redeye bound for Beijing lifted off from runway 32R at Kuala Lumpur International Airport. As its landing gear curled up into its belly, the Boeing 777 climbed through 2,000 feet, then banked to the right and leveled out as it rose into the starry night.

Twenty-seven minutes later, Malaysia Airlines Flight 370 crossed the east coast of the Malay Peninsula at 35,000 feet and headed out to sea. Cruising into a light headwind, it clocked a ground speed of approximately 470 knots. Soon after, it approached the edge of Malaysian-monitored airspace.

When a plane transitions from one zone of control to another, the controller calls up the plane on the radio and gives the pilot the name and radio frequency of the authority he or she will be speaking to next. And so, 38 minutes after takeoff, the following exchange took place:

LUMPUR RADAR: Malaysian Three Seven Zero contact Ho Chi Minh 120 decimal 9. Good Night.

MH370: Good Night, Malaysian Three Seven Zero.

The plane was operating normally, and the weather was fair. The moon was just setting; the sun would not rise for another six hours. Far below, a warm breeze ruffled the surface of the South China Sea. Two minutes after the final transmission, the plane passed the last waypoint in Malaysia, a spot named IGARI, and turned slightly to the right, heading toward its next navigational fix inside Vietnamese airspace.

Five seconds later, the radar signal on the controller's screen winked out. To this day, no one can say precisely what had gone wrong. The stars continued to shine, the wind continued to blow. But the plane was no longer on its route.

* * *

Inside the tower at Ho Chi Minh City's Tan Son Nhat airport, controllers were working the graveyard shift. When inbound flights are stacked up, air traffic control is a fast-paced, high-stakes game of 3D chess. Not tonight. From time to time, one of the controllers would get on the radio to acknowledge a plane's arrival or give it a new altitude clearance. But mostly, they just watched clusters of numbers inch across the screen, as time unspooled in that glacial middle-of-the-night way.

At 1:21am local time, the controllers were expecting MH370 to enter their control zone. A minute passed, and there was still no sign of it. This was odd: modern commercial aircraft operate with an extreme precision enabled by satellite navigation, computer control, and atomic clocks. Routes are planned and flown with laserlike accuracy. The plane should have been visible by a number of electronic means. Its transponder, a system called ADS-B, a messaging system called ACARS—all three should have continuously been sending information about the plane to ground control. But all three had fallen silent as the plane left Malaysian airspace.

Now three minutes had passed. By international convention, the Ho Chi Minh City controllers were supposed to start calling their counterparts in the neighboring air traffic control zones to find out what had happened to the plane. But tonight that didn't seem necessary. There was surely a reasonable explanation for the hiccup. Five minutes went by, then ten. Nothing. Fifteen minutes. This was getting ridiculous.

Finally, at 1:39am, a controller picked up the landline to Kuala Lumpur and reported that they still hadn't heard from MH370. Kuala Lumpur advised that they couldn't see it on their screens, either. Two minutes later, Ho Chi Minh City called again and asked if the plane had turned back into Malaysian airspace. The answer was no.

Very strange. For twenty minutes, both Kuala Lumpur and Ho Chi Minh City kept radioing the plane, but neither got a response. Over the next few hours, with increasing urgency, air traffic controllers around the region phoned back and forth to one another, and to the airline, trying to establish where the plane might have gone.

At first, the airline's operations center reported that their tracking system showed that the plane was over Cambodia. After some confused calls to Phnom Penh, the airline realized that its software was wrong. The plane wasn't there, either.

At 5.20am, a Malaysia Airlines staffer asked a Kuala Lumpur controller whether the plane had been successfully handed off to Ho Chi Minh City. The controller had to wake up his supervisor to ask. Ten minutes later, the supervisor activated a search-and-rescue response. In Beijing, relatives arriving to meet their loved ones received grim news: MH370 was missing.

Soon news of the disappearance was ricocheting around the global media sphere. This was big. It wasn't just that 227 passengers and 12 crew were missing and possibly dead. There was a whiff of strangeness. Commercial airliners don't just disappear. The 777 in particular is an advanced and extremely robust airplane. Introduced by Boeing in the 1990s, it was the company's first fly-by-wire airplane, controlled entirely by a powerful computer system. The aircraft had proven remarkably safe. No 777 had ever suffered an inflight mishap before. What could have gone wrong?

In the days that followed, no clear answers emerged. Nor did they in the following weeks, months, or years. Distilling a set of possible flight paths from a handful of clues, search officials launched a long and intensive effort to scan a remote swath of seabed in the southern Indian Ocean. They found nothing.

For a time, the disappearance of MH370 was the biggest story in the world. Millions of people found themselves obsessed. In an age of 24/7 global connectivity it seemed inconceivable that a state-of-the art airliner could simply vanish. Speculation and conspiracy theories swirled. Today, half a decade later, little has changed. The public remains baffled, and the authorities can offer no credible explanation.

It's an oft-voiced fear that the mystery of MH370 will never be solved. Having pored over every emerging detail since the day the plane went missing, however, I don't share that point of view. While all of the evidence is circumstantial, and much of it is highly technical in nature, there is a considerable amount of it. Taken together it allows us to piece together the circumstances of the incident in some detail.

People have a natural yearning for simple solutions. Occam's razor, they say. But if there is one thing that has become abundantly clear about MH370, it is that the solution is neither simple nor easy. In order to gain useful insight, we must roll up our sleeves and dive deep into the science and mathematics underpinning the evidence. We must take detours into such seeming arcana as prefrequency calibration algorithms, Bayes' theorem, and the lifecycles of goose barnacles and tube worms.

Having dived headlong into this technical minutiae, I can report that once all the noise and fog is cleared away, there is only one plausible explanation for what happened to the missing plane. It is no exaggeration to say that the story it reveals stretches our understanding of what human beings are capable of, both technologically and morally.

2.
MARCH 10, 2014

I don't remember where I was when I first heard about MH370. As a science journalist and a private pilot, I write about aviation a lot, and half the time that means covering crashes. I do remember, however, the moment I fell into the bottomless hole. I was sitting in my car on the Upper West Side of Manhattan, waiting for my parking spot to become legal. I took out my phone and checked my email. An editor at Slate, the online magazine, had written to ask if I would write about the Malaysian airliner that had gone missing. I tapped out a response accepting her offer, with mixed emotions—I was already past deadline on a story about helicopters for *Popular Mechanics*.

"The most telling detail so far," I wrote, "being the total absence of automatic signals sent by the plane. So things either became catastrophic very quickly (bomb?) or the automatic reporting was turned off deliberately or ... ? (Crazy question: Do we even know for sure that it has crashed?)"

By the time I filed my copy, that question seemed less crazy. Search and rescue teams had spent the better part of a week looking for wreckage and hadn't found a trace.

In my article, I enumerated the electronic systems that a plane uses to stay in touch with the outside world, and described a case from a few years before that bore some eerie similarities. On June 1, 2009, Air France Flight 447 from Rio de Janeiro to Paris crashed in the middle of the Atlantic Ocean. Because its flight crew had already said goodbye to air traffic controllers in Brazil, and were still out of radar range of controllers in Africa, it was many hours before anyone realized the plane was missing. MH370, too, had vanished between zones of control. In this case, however, the gap between contacts was much smaller: a matter of minutes, rather than hours. Was the resemblance just bad luck? Or did it suggest that someone had maliciously exploited the gap?

My *Slate* piece ran on March 12th. At 6am the next morning I went on CNN. Before I knew it, I was going on air as many as six times a day. Network head Jeff Zucker had decided the network would go all in. Producers wound up trying to book pretty much anyone who'd ever written or talked about airplanes. As time went by they winnowed their expert pool down to a dozen or so regulars who earned the title "CNN aviation analyst": airline pilots, ex-government honchos, aviation lawyers, and me. We'd appear solo, or in pairs, or larger groups for panel discussions—whatever it took to vary the rhythm of the perpetual chatter.

There was plenty to talk about. The story just

kept getting stranger. Malaysian officials revealed, then denied, then finally admitted that their military had tracked the plane for an hour after it disappeared from air traffic controllers' radar screens just five seconds after passing the last waypoint in Malaysian airspace. Evidently someone had turned off the plane's electronic communication systems, but the plane had still been visible to the so-called "primary" radar used in air defense. The system had watched as MH370 pulled a U-turn so aggressive that it must have been flown manually. It then climbed and accelerated to the limit of its flight envelope as it headed back across the Malay Peninsula before turning northwest and flying up the middle of the Malacca Strait toward the Andaman Islands. But at 18:22 Universal Time (2:22am local time), 60 nautical miles north of the western tip of Sumatra, it reached the limits of the system's range and the signal winked out.

In effect, MH370 had disappeared twice: once from air traffic control radar, and then again an hour later from military radar.

This revelation changed the picture dramatically. Suddenly the disappearance didn't look at all like an accident. The plane had not circled or followed a twisting path, as it would if maneuvering for an emergency landing; nor had it headed unswervingly on a single course, like a plane on autopilot whose human pilots had become incapacitated through smoke inhalation or cockpit depressurization. It had flown a zig-zag series of segments from waypoint to waypoint, implying that whoever was in control understood how to operate and navigate a commercial aircraft. What's more, the plane had flown quickly, faster than planes normally cruise. Malaysian authorities realized that what they were dealing with was clearly a deliberate act. Someone had taken the plane. But who? To me, the fact that the plane had gone dark just five seconds after leaving Malaysian airspace, and then had turned around in what looked to be a high-performance maneuver, implied that whoever was in control of the plane had an advanced understanding of both airliner operations and air traffic surveillance. Either the plane had been taken by its own flight crew, or it had been commandeered by sophisticated hijackers.

Of the two possibilities, initial evidence strongly favored the first. Only one minute had elapsed between the calmly enunciated "Goodnight, Malaysia 370" and the start of the 180-degree turn. That's very little time for hijackers to get through a locked cockpit door, overpower the flight crew, turn off all communications equipment, and reprogram the flight computer. And anyway, how could hijackers do all that without the flight crew sending out a distress signal? It seemed much more plausible that either the captain or the co-pilot had absconded with the plane.

Digesting the new evidence, officials moved the priority search area from the South China Sea to the Indian Ocean, focusing their efforts near MH370's last known position over the western end of the Malacca Strait.

But their work there had scarcely begun when another bombshell dropped.

3.
MARCH 15, 2014

The new revelation had to do with the plane's satellite communication system. Because radar and radio don't work once a plane is more than a few hundred miles from the nearest ground-based antenna, airliners are equipped with radio antennas that can link with satellites orbiting above the equator. As these satellites orbit the Earth exactly once per day, they effectively remain in a fixed position relative to the surface. MH370 was communicating with a satellite called 3F-1 that was operated by the London-based firm Inmarsat.

On March 15, Malaysian prime minister Najib Razak held a press conference to confirm rumors that had been circulating for days: that Inmarsat's computers had logged a series of signals automatically exchanged between MH370 and 3F-1 after the plane had disappeared from military radar.

Airlines primarily use Inmarsat's service to carry phone calls and electronic data such as text messages. The signals received from MH370, however, did not contain any such information; whoever was in control of the plane during those last six hours did not intentionally use the satcom system to contact the outside world.

The system is designed, however, such that if a user remains inactive for a certain amount of time—in this case, an hour—then Inmarsat's ground station automatically transmits a brief signal to see if the user is still logged on. Inmarsat calls such signals "electronic handshakes" or "pings." If there is no reply, then the user is presumed to have either turned the system off or to have left the coverage area. But that's not what happened in the case of MH370. For six hours after it vanished from primary radar, its satcom system kept responding.

Even though the handshakes' content offered no insight into what was happening aboard the plane, their mere existence proved that the plane had not crashed in the vicinity of the Malacca Strait, as had been widely presumed, but stayed aloft for quite a long time. Long enough, indeed, to have flown 3000 nautical miles or more.

In which direction, though? Unfortunately, Malaysia Airlines did not subscribe to Inmarsat's premium brand of service, SwiftBroadband, which automatically includes position data in all its signals. Instead, the airline subscribed to a cheaper version called ClassicAero, and because of that the transmissions logged by Inmarsat contained no information such as location, speed, or altitude. They did, however, include metadata—that is to say, data about the data—such as the time each transmission was sent, the frequency at which it was received, and so forth. One of the parameters they had logged was something called the Burst Timing Offset, or BTO, a measure of the time elapsed between the satellite's query and the plane's reply.

Because light travels at a finite speed, and the plane's electronics require a certain amount of time to generate a response, there's always a gap in time that correlates with the physical distance between the plane and the satellite. The set of all the points on the earth's surface which lie at this precise distance from the satellite makes a ring. If you exclude the portions of the ring to which the plane could not possibly have flown because they lie too far away, what you have left is an arc.

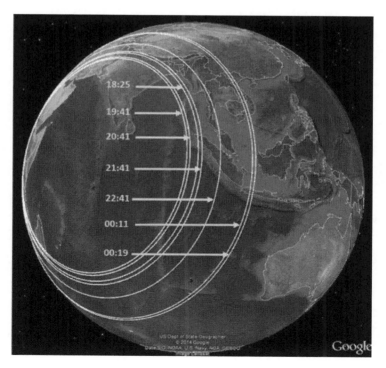

During its last six hours MH370 transmitted seven pings. The plane presumably ended its flight somewhere near the last one—the 7th arc—an enormous curve that runs from Central Asia through China, Vietnam, and Indonesia and winds up in the ocean west of Australia.

How to even contemplate searching such a vast area? As they thought about it, Imarsat scientists realized that the plane was much more likely to be on some parts of the arc than others.

Imagine that you have two ping rings, one created an hour after the other. The rings are basically concentric, with the second ring's radius 300 nautical miles bigger than the first. Let's say the plane started at some arbitrary point on the innermost ring. If that's all we know, then the plane could have taken any of an infinite number of routes from the first to the second. It could have travelled radially directly outward at average speed of 300 knots. Or, if traveling at an average speed of 400 knots, it could have turned left or right at an angle.

Assuming a certain speed allows you to draw a path between each successive set of arcs with a particular endpoint on the 7th arc. This technique has a somewhat surprising and important feature: due to the directional ambiguity of the BTO data, every route created in this way has a mirror-image route lying in the opposite direction. For instance, if you plot a route of gradually decreasing speed that curves off to the south, there will always exist an equally valid route that curves off to the north.

Given the plane's last known position and assuming a likely speed of about 500 miles per hour, experts reasoned that the plane's most likely endpoint lay at either the northernmost or southernmost extremities of the 7th arc.

Many journalists, including most of my fellow aviation analysts on CNN, thought the southern option more likely. After all, if the plane had gone north into the teeming heart of Asia, wouldn't someone have picked it up on radar? The authorities agreed, and so a search was begun in the southern Indian Ocean under the auspices of the Australian Transport Safety Board (ATSB). Ships and planes from 14 countries scanned the ocean surface in what amounted to the largest search-and-rescue operation in history.

But for me, there was a big problem with the southern option. If the plane went south, then everyone on board must have died, and my gut was telling me that whoever carried this out was too talented and motivated to quietly snuff themselves.

With so much still unknown about the case, I found it easy to imagine all sorts of dark scenarios. Since no one had yet claimed responsibility, I wondered if the perpetrators were readying the plane in secret for a 9-11-style attack. Since most of the passengers were Chinese, it seemed to me that separatist Uighurs would be likely culprits.

I wrote another article for *Slate*, positing that Malaysia's announcement meant that "the plane ended its flight in a restive part of Central Asia." This was quite different from what most other commentators were saying, and my editor was reluctant. I promised her that if I turned out to be wrong I would write a follow-up piece explaining my error and accepting responsibility.

4.

MARCH 25, 2014

As I was heading into CNN the third Tuesday after the disappearance, I received a text from a producer: the Malaysian prime minister, Najib Razak, was about to hold another press conference to discuss "developments." My heart skipped a beat. Had they found the plane? I arrived at the Time Warner Center to find the studio abuzz. Maybe this long saga was about to draw to a close. But when Najib at last appeared at the podium, what he announced was something no one had anticipated. Yes, he declared, the fate of the plane had been determined. It had indeed gone south. But there were no bodies and no debris. Inmarsat, in concert with the UK's Air Accidents Investigation Branch (AAIB), had made the determination through the power of mathematics alone.

Based on their new analysis, Inmarsat and the AAIB have concluded that MH370 flew along the southern corridor, and that its last position was somewhere in the middle of the Indian Ocean west of Perth. This is a remote region, far from any possible landing sites. It is therefore with deep sadness and regret that I must inform you that, according to this new data, flight MH370 ended in the southern Indian Ocean.

Never before in history had hundreds of people essentially been declared dead without any evidence but an undisclosed numerical analysis of undisclosed data. From within the hotel briefing room, onlookers could hear the wails of family members in a nearby room.

Was it really possible to reach such a conclusion based on math alone? Many of the missing passengers' family members were skeptical. They marched in protest to the Malaysian embassy in Beijing, where they hurled water bottles and battled with paramilitary soldiers in riot gear.

To justify the conclusion, Malaysia's acting transport minister held yet another press conference at which he released a report summarizing Inmarsat's analysis.

This time the metadata under discussion was not the Burst Timing Offset, but another parameter called the Burst Frequency Offset, or BFO. Just as the motion of a speeding train makes the pitch of its whistle go up or down—the Doppler effect—the relative motion of a satellite and an airplane shifts the frequency of radio signals transmitted between them. The BFO is a measure of this difference. Inmarsat was able to calculate what BFO values they would expect to see if the plane flew to the north versus what they would see if it flew to the south. They found that the observed values were much closer to the calculated southern values than to the calculated northern ones.

The explanation made sense in principle, and the graphs and charts looked solidly scientific, but none of us in the green room understood exactly how these calculations worked. Nor, for that matter, did any engineers I knew. No one had ever before used BFO values to try to determine the location of a missing plane.

Torie, my editor, asked if I was ready to write the apology piece I'd promised. I asked her to hang fire. So far the Malaysians had refused to release the complete Inmarsat data logs or to explain exactly how the scientists' calculations had worked. I argued that until the details were released, it would be irresponsible to rubber-stamp their conclusions. I asked her to give me some time to try to verify what the prime minister had said.

Fortunately, I had recently acquired a new group of friends who could help me do just that. In between going on CNN and writing for Slate, I'd started posting more technical MH370 material on my website, jeffwise.net. I'd launched the blog a few years before as a place to post short items about science and aviation, but had only attracted a small readership. Each post usually got only two or three comments. Once MH370 happened, it was a whole new game; each post might now get three or four hundred comments.

Many of the new readers had serious engineering

chops and contributed information I couldn't have found any other way. Among them was Mike Exner, a veteran of the satellite communications industry who'd done pioneering work on the first GPS systems. Exner led me to a New Zealand space scientist named Duncan Steel who a few days earlier had begun posting details of the Inmarsat satellite's orbital mechanics on a website of his own. Steel's site and mine both grew into busy forums for technically savvy MH370 obsessives. If you found yourself wondering how a geosynchronous satellite responds to a shortage of hydrazine, or what a Boeing 777 Flight Management System does after it reaches its last entered waypoint, all you had to do was ask.

Around the globe, a loose association of independent researchers went to work, mining the March 25 report for clues that we could use to reverse-engineer the full Inmarsat data set. As emails whizzed back and forth, someone came up with the idea of giving ourselves a name: the Independent Group. The puzzle was daunting, but the prospect of crowd-sourcing a solution to the world's greatest aviation mystery was exhilarating.

5.

APRIL 2014

Malaysia's revelation that the plane must have gone south effectively put the investigation in the hands of Australia, which by international treaty is responsible for search-and-rescue operations in that part of the Indian Ocean. After weighing the evidence, the ATSB decided to focus on a 23,000-square-mile area west of Perth. Ships and planes spotted many pieces of debris on the surface, provoking a frenzy of "Breaking News" banners, but none of it turned out to be from an airplane. Another week went by, and the ATSB shifted the search area 600 miles to the north. Later it would move the search area further south again. All this rejiggering was confusing, but it gave us CNN talking heads something to chatter about on air.

Mainly, though, we waited for the big news: the discovery of the first piece of confirmed debris. It seemed certain to happen any day now. Where one piece was found, others would be found nearby; by "drifting" the debris—that is, modeling the currents that had moved them around—investigators would be able to determine a likely area of impact. The wreckage would lie directly beneath the impact point.

Once the wreckage was found, the mystery's solution would be at hand. Amid the scattered debris, investigators would find the aircraft's two black boxes. (Though they are called "black" their color is really international orange.) The first, the Flight Data Recorder, or FDR, contains thousands of parameters such as airspeed, altitude, and position. The other, the Cockpit Voice Recorder, or CVR, preserves flight-deck audio for the final two hours of flight. To make these crucial devices easier to locate, they are built with acoustic pingers that generate an ultrasonic signal when immersed in water.

Once the approximate location of the plane's resting place was identified, searchers would drag a kind of high-tech underwater microphone called a Towed Pinger Locator (TPL) back and forth listening for the acoustic pingers. The gear's range is about a mile, so searchers would be able to sweep a relatively large area quickly. Once they detected the pinger, robot submarines would be dispatched to take pictures of the wreckage and bring the black boxes to the surface.

A problem was looming, however. Pingers' batteries are only designed to last for 30 days, and that deadline was fast approaching. If the batteries died before the black boxes were found, locating the wreckage would become vastly more difficult.

In what amounted to a Hail Mary pass, the authorities decided to put the listening gear in the water without having yet found any floating debris.

On April 4, an Australian naval ship deployed a TPL. Mirabile dictu: The very next day, the ship detected a faint signal. Hours later, another signal was detected 1.2 miles from the first. Then two more, a few miles away. It was a moment of enormous relief. After weeks of frustration, the answer to the riddle was at hand. The Malaysian minister of transport, Hishmmuddin Hussein, declared that he was "cautiously hopeful that there will be a positive development in the next few days, if not hours." Search officials were upbeat, and so was the crowd in the CNN green room. Everyone was ready to bring this tragic saga to a definitive conclusion.

The only Debbie Downer was me. I found this mind-boggling stroke of luck implausible, and pointed out that the pings detected were at the wrong frequency, and were located too far apart to have plausibly been generated by black boxes sitting stationary on the seabed. For the next two weeks, I was the odd man out on Don Lemon's six-guest panel blocks, gleefully savaged by my fellow on-air experts.

The Australians deployed an underwater robot called a Bluefin 21 to scan the seabed and find the source of the pings. They started in the area of maximum probability, so with every day that went by, the chance that they'd find anything dropped. After two weeks, the Bluefin 21 had searched the entire seabed within detection range of the pingers. There was nothing there.

By the rules of TV news, the issue wasn't settled until an official said it was. But nerves were wearing thin. One night, an underwater search veteran agreed with me that the so-called acoustic ping detections had to be false. Backstage after the show, he and another aviation analyst nearly came to blows. "You don't know what you're talking about! I've done extensive research!" the other analyst shouted. "There's nothing else those pings could be!"

Eventually, the pinger story petered out the way most stories do: the producers just stopped scheduling segments about it. A month later, a US Navy officer said publicly that the pings had not come from MH370 after all.

The Australians called off the surface search. "It is highly unlikely at this stage that we will find any aircraft debris on the ocean surface," said Prime Minister Tony Abbott. "By this stage... most material would have become waterlogged and sunk."

It had been 52 days since the plane had gone missing, Millions of dollars had been spent to absolutely no effect.

For me, the acoustic pings offered an important lesson: the search authorities, and a large proportion of the media, did not have a reliable mastery of the story's technical details. Until irrefutable evidence was in hand, every official pronouncement would have to be carefully fact-checked.

6.
MAY 2014

My CNN bookings were winding down, but my obsession with the case kept growing. There was so much to chew on, with new leads emerging on multiple fronts. In the wake of the acoustic-pinger debacle, the authorities felt mounting pressure to release more information, especially from the impassioned and increasingly well-organized family members of the missing passengers. At last, on May 27, the Malaysians released the raw Inmarsat data.

Working together, the scattered legion of amateur experts swan-dived into the 47-page trove. Much of the data turned out to be irrelevant, but all seven handshakes were depicted in great detail, and some other intriguing clues were revealed as well. One of the most surprising, and significant, was that the satellite communications system had not inadvertently been left on, as many of us had presumed, but had instead somehow become disconnected and then logged back on. This event had taken place at 18:25 Universal Time (UTC), just three minutes after the plane had disappeared from radar. Could this have happened accidentally, or was it further evidence of deliberate action by hijackers? Answering that question would be a priority in the months to come.

Also highly significant were two brief sentences in the explanatory note that accompanied the data: "Inmarsat Classic Aero mobile terminals are designed to correct for aircraft Doppler effect on their transmit signals. The terminal type used on MH370 assumes a stationary satellite at a fixed orbital position." At last, this told us why officials believed the plane had gone south instead of north.

Here's the short version:

As it looks down from its orbit, an Inmarsat satellite has a line of sight to literally billions of radio-frequency devices, from cell-phones and walkie talkies to radio stations and radar dishes. In order to avoid getting swamped by all that babble, the airplane signal must land within the narrow band of the spectrum that's been reserved for it. Very, very narrow: the frequency has to be accurate to within parts per billion.

To find this window, satellite communications engineers grapple with a lot of sources of frequency error, one of them being the Doppler effect. To compensate for it, a piece of equipment within the airplane called the Satellite Data Unit (SDU) uses the aircraft's position and speed to calculate the anticipated Doppler shift, then adds or subtracts this amount from the frequency at which it transmits to the satellite so the incoming signal hits at just the right frequency. Satellite companies routinely track and log the frequency so that they can fix any problems that might arise, and that's why Inmarsat was able to turn over MH370's BFO data to search officials.

The SDU is located above the ceiling of the passenger cabin, right below the satellite antenna, which protrudes from the top of the airplane. Imagine an electronic version of an old-timey ham radio operator sitting underneath a radio tower. The SDU doesn't generate information per se; it's just providing the link between the aircraft and the satellite. You can think of it as somewhat analagous to a smartphone. When you turn on a phone, it connects to the cell network, but it doesn't communicate with anyone until you send a text message, make a call, or activate an app.

What the new report told us was that MH370's SDU was programmed to assume that the satellite was orbiting over a fixed position at the equator. But in fact, 3F-1's orbit had a slight wobble. Launched in 1996, it was intended to operate only for 13 years. As it aged, it ran low on the fuel that it required to stay precisely on location. The satellite's wobble caused the plane's electronics to incorrectly compensate for its own velocity and thereby left a trace of that motion hidden in the BFO value.

Just after the plane disappeared from radar, the satellite's wobble would have made a northbound plane's transmission frequency too high. Then, after a few hours, the frequency would have fallen. Conversely, if the plane had flown south, the frequency would have been too low at first, and then risen. This latter pattern is precisely what Inmarsat scientists saw in their retrieved MH370 data.

I spent a week playing with spreadsheets, running the numbers again and again until there was no doubt in my mind: the scientists had been right after all. The Inmarsat data did unambiguously show that the plane had flown south, not north, after it disappeared from primary radar.

As promised, I wrote a piece for *Slate* explaining why I'd been wrong.

7.
JUNE 2014

Apart from precipitating my mortifying public climb-down, the release of the Inmarsat data was a thrilling development, dangling the possibility that with some elbow grease and a bit of mathematical savvy, we could crack the case. Since the BFO contained information about how the aircraft had been moving, it should allow us to figure out where on the 7th arc the plane had been at the time of the last ping. The wreckage of the plane should lie somewhere in the vicinity.

Everyone set to work generating routes that matched the ping rings, then calculating how closely these routes matched the observed BFO data. Each time one of us came up with a route that seemed like a good fit, we would email it around to everyone else. I spent days working through the details of a route that ran through a waypoint southwest of the Cocos Islands and ended up around 38° south latitude. Was it the right one? It turned out to be impossible to tell from just the data at hand. As Mark Dickinson, Vice

President of Satellite Operations at Inmarsat, later put it to me, "If you know the state of the aircraft, you can predict what the BFO is going to be, but if you only have the BFO number, it's much harder to reverse engineer out all the components that make up that number."

Nevertheless, we found that all of our routes ended up in a cluster. A sense of excitement grew: if each of us was independently coming up with more or less the same answer, it most likely was correct.

Our efforts got a boost with the June 26 publication of a new report by the ATSB called "MH370 — Definition of Underwater Search Areas." It explained how the Australians had used the Inmarsat data to delineate a search area. One revelation in particular seemed particularly important. It was in a paragraph about the 18:25 log-on request:

> A log-on request in the middle of a flight is not common and can occur for only a few reasons. These include a power interruption to the aircraft satellite data unit (SDU), a software failure, loss of critical systems providing input to the SDU or a loss of the link due to aircraft attitude. An analysis was performed which determined that the characteristics and timing of the logon requests were best matched as resulting from power interruption to the SDU.

This was a massive twist. When we'd first heard about the Inmarsat data, we assumed that it had been generated because the satcom had been left on accidentally when everything else had been turned off. Then we'd found out that it had actually reconnected with the satellite a few minutes after the plane left radar coverage. But we didn't know how or why that could have happened. Now the ATSB was saying that most likely the power to the SDU had been cut and then restored.

It was only because of this reboot that investigators had the seven Inmarsat pings. Everything we knew about the last six hours of the plane's flight was derived from those pings. If we didn't fully understand the reboot itself, everything else was built on sand. We needed to figure out how the power interruption had occurred.

The question turned out to be a tough one. Airplane manufacturers keep a tight lid on the technical details of their airplanes, lest competitors steal their secrets. But by scouring the web, reaching out through personal connections, and tapping our own expertise, the independent researchers were able to piece together a comprehensive answer.

What we found is that there is no on/off switch for the SDU in a 777 cockpit. In normal aircraft operation, it simply comes on when the plane's electrical system is turned on. A person wanting to turn off the SDU has two options. The first is to go to the business-class cabin, open an unlocked floor hatch near the galley, descend into a compartment called the electronics and equipment bay (or E/E bay), and flip three circuit breakers. I call this the "easy way."

The second method, which can be accomplished directly from the cockpit, is to isolate a portion of the the plane's electrical system called the left AC bus. The SDU gets its power from this bus, so if the bus is depowered, the SDU shuts off, too. I call this the "hard way" to turn off the SDU because it involves throwing a series of circuit breakers on the overhead panel in an order that requires a good deal of technical knowledge.

It's also hard in the sense that, because a big chunk of a 777's electronics are connected to the left AC bus, shutting it down results in the loss of a whole bunch of systems, many of which are likely unknown to anyone who isn't a Boeing employee. It's possible that one of the pilots had cooked up a plan that involved temporarily switching off some other component connected to the left AC bus, and in so doing accidentally depowered and repowered the SDU. But after much discussion, neither I nor anybody else could think of a component you'd want to do that to.

I turned to Patrick Smith, a 777 pilot who is one of the most respected aviation commentators in the United States, for his opinion about the SDU reboot. He replied, "The what?" After I explained, he answered: "There isn't a 777 pilot alive, I'll bet you, who has the remotest clue as to what the SDU is." I asked many other 777 pilots and have gotten a similar response.

This struck me as highly significant. If rebooting of the SDU was something that no normal airline pilot can conceive of, let alone carry out, then whoever had taken the plane must have been highly sophisticated.

It also left me puzzled as to motive. Why would a

sophisticated hijacker, one who had just committed an aggressive evasion and managed to escape from radar coverage, want to turn on a piece of equipment that apparently would serve no purpose for him, but which could give away his location?

In the end, I was able to come up with no good simple reason. But it occurred to me that there might be a complicated one. Might it perhaps be possible, I wondered, for a clever perpetrator to tamper with the SDU in such a way that it produced misleading metadata? If that were the case, the plane could be made to leave behind a trail of false electronic breadcrumbs implying that the plane had flown off into the remote Indian Ocean when in fact it had turned and gone another way.

If that were the case, then the reboot of the SDU at 18:25 might not have been a failure in the hijacker's elaborate evasion plan, but its *pièce de resistance.*

8.

THE SPOOF

When the idea that the Inmarsat data might have been maliciously altered first occurred to me, I almost dismissed it as preposterous. First and foremost, it would require the perpetrators to be almost inconceivably clever. If airline pilots don't know about the SDU, then presumably only a tiny number of people in the entire aviation industry would have the chops to contemplate such a deed.

On the other hand, experts within the investigation apparently didn't find the idea inconceivable. In an interview with the BBC, Inmarsat engineer Alan Schuster-Bruce said that after he and his colleagues completed their first analysis of the BFO data, "one of the concerns we had was in fact this could just be a big hoax that someone had played on Inmarsat."

They mostly convinced themselves that that wasn't the case, but a lingering doubt remained. As Inmarsat VP Aviation David Coiley put it: "We are very confident that this data is correct assuming that there is no other way this data has been spoofed."

I couldn't get the thought out of my head. So I decided to see if such a thing were even possible. First, I needed to learn more about how the BTO and BFO values are generated. Mike Exner, the Independent Group member with expertise in satellite communications, gave me the lowdown.

The BTO values, he explained, are a function of two things: the distance between the plane and the satellite, and internal processes that take place entirely within the SDU. As such, the BTO data would be extremely difficult to tamper with. What's more, Inmarsat had only within the past year begun logging those values, so it's unlikely that a perpetrator wanting to mislead investigators would even know that they were being stored.

BFO values, on the other hand, were potentially quite interesting. Exner explained that the SDU obtains the speed and location data it needs to perform the Doppler precompensation algorithm via a 1/8" cable connected to the E/E bay, where a box called the Inertial Reference System (or IRS) calculates the plane's location and velocity. If those incoming values could be changed, so could the BFO values. And any satcom engineer would know that Inmarsat was logging its BFO data because they're important for maintaining the network.

As I've mentioned before, the E/E bay is accessible during flight through an unlocked hatch at the front of the first-class cabin. (At least, on all planes built by Boeing; on Airbus planes this hatch is inside the cockpit.) If you were to climb down into the E/E bay and disconnect the SDU cable from the

IRS, you could plug it into an electronic device capable of generating false position information. (Such gear would have to be manufactured from scratch; "there are certainly no commercial, off-the-shelf boxes like that," said Exner.) In essence, the signal would be lying to the SDU about where the plane was located and how fast it was going, causing the SDU to transmit at an incorrect frequency. If you knew how the satellite communication business worked, you would know that Inmarsat computers would automatically log this information, and that in all likelihood Inmarsat engineers would later find it—and be misled. You would have created a false trail of breadcrumbs.

But why? Well, if a plane simply disappears in the middle of nowhere, with absolutely no clues, that's suspicious. The authorities would assume foul play, sound all alarms, and search in all directions. But if pursuers had a trail to focus on—in this case, one that led off into the middle of the deep blue ocean —they'd never think to question it. The clue, once perceived, would be subtle, so arcane, that the investigators would congratulate themselves for their brilliance in finding it and discerning its meaning. The magician Teller has pointed out a quirk of human psychology can be exploited by practitioners of stage deception: "When a magician lets you notice something on your own, his lie becomes impenetrable."

Remember Operation Mincemeat? In 1943, a fisherman found the body of a British officer floating off the Spanish coast. The authorities turned the corpse over to German intelligence, who found it to be loaded with secret documents, including one indicating that the expected Allied assault from North Africa would target Sardinia, not Sicily, as widely presumed. Every detail vouched for the authenticity of the documents, from the dead man's clothes to the array of accompanying possessions. These included several love letters, a photo of the man's fiancée, a bill from an exclusive London tailor, and a theater ticket stub. Either this man and his belongings had all been meticulously forged, or he really was who he seemed to be. Hitler himself was utterly convinced.

Hitler was wrong, however. The whole thing was a ruse, an elaborate deception cooked up with painstaking care by British intelligence. Because of its success the Germans shifted three divisions to Sardinia, the invasion landed at Sicily, and the war was that much closer to being over.

Given the oddities surrounding the case, I wondered if MH370 might represent a deception crafted at the same level of sophistication.

For this to be true, however, a very specific set of criteria would have to be met. As we've seen, the hijacked plane would have to be a Boeing, not an Airbus. It would have to be a fly-by-wire 777 or a 787, not one of Boeing's earlier planes which used mechanical control systems. The airline would have to have subscribed to the low-cost version of Inmarsat's service, Classic Aero, and not its high-end version, Swift Broadband (the latter automatically incorporates GPS location data into the signal). The plane's route after disappearing would have to have been entirely under the footprint of an aging

Inmarsat satellite in a decaying orbit. And the implied direction would have to be toward an oceanic basin in which the plane could be "lost."

It just so happens that MH370 meets all these criteria.

The fact that the E/E bay is freely accessible could also explain how MH370 could have been taken over so quickly after the final radio transmission. Inside the E/E bay, you have full access to the systems that control every function of the plane. "An individual in the avionics bay could potentially disable all communications as well as disable control from the cockpit," Victor Iannello, an Independent Group member from Virginia, told me. "He or she could have complete control of the aircraft and the crew would be helpless."

The security implications of leaving the plane's nerve center freely accessible have not gone unnoticed. Matt Wuillemin, an Australian former 777 pilot, wrote a master's thesis on the vulnerability in June 2013. In his thesis, Wuillemin notes that in addition to the Flight Control Computers, the E/E bay also houses the oxygen cylinders that supply the flight crews' masks in case of a depressurization event, as well as the controls for the system that locks the flight deck door. "Information is publicly available online describing the cockpit defences and systems located within this compartment," Wuillemin notes. "This hatch may therefore be accessible inflight to a knowledgeable and malevolent passenger with catastrophic consequences."

Wuillemin penned his warning less than a year before MH370 disappeared.

9.
JULY 2014

In order for such an attack to take place, someone would have to have been on board to carry it out. We'd known since March that if the plane didn't go south, it went north, to Kazakhstan. Kazakhstan's president, the Soviet-era strongman Nursultan Nazarbayev, is a close ally of Vladimir Putin's. He was the only national leader who publicly supported Russia's annexation of Crimea in March 2014.

Kazakhstan itself lacks the technical savvy to carry out a sophisticated hijack, but the same is not true of Russia. Russia's aerospace industry builds and operates a variety of military jets, commercial aircraft and satellites. In some ways, Russian capabilities outstrip America's; since 2011 the US has relied entirely on Russia to launch its astronauts into space. So it would be foolish to imagine that tampering with BFO values would be beyond the Kremlin's capabilities. "Messing with satellite data is very doable for the Russians," former CIA agent Robert Baer told me.

Kazakhstan is home to the Baikonur Cosmodrome, a 2,593 square mile territory leased by Russia and used for launching space rockets. It has two runways suitable for landing a 777 on, including one in a remote stretch of desert, far from prying eyes. Russia has other facilities within Kazakhstan as well, including an important military radar facility and a missile-testing range. Another possible landing spot would be the Kazakh airbase at Zhetigen, which is located less than 20 miles past the 7th arc.

If Russia did take the plane, who aboard might have been a hijacker? I studied the passenger manifest with an eye for the sort of person who might carry out a covert operation. My model was Igor Girkin, a character described by a Reuters article in May. Girkin was a 43-year-old GRU officer who took charge of the separatist Donetsk People's Republic under the nom-de-guerre of Colonel Strelkov. Before he went off to war, he'd blended seamlessly into civilian life, just another guy who headed to work in a jacket and tie every morning. "He's always been very polite and very quiet, though I didn't know him well," one neighbor told Reuters. "Nothing about him was particularly outstanding."

"The Russian security apparatus have something that they call the 'active reserve,'" Mark Galeotti, a professor of global affairs at NYU, explained to me. "Basically, you've left the security apparatus on the surface, they've probably placed you in a job, and as well as being paid for that job, you're also receiving a retainer, with the understanding that at some point— it's like the mafia, really—at some point they're going to come and ask something of you."

There was only one Russian aboard MH370, a 43-year-old businessman from Irkutsk named Nikolai Brodsky. Brodsky was sitting in business class seat 3K, approximately 12 feet from the E/E bay hatch. Back in economy class were two Ukrainians of Russian ethnicity, Sergei Deineka and Oleg Chustrak. The men, both 45, were sitting together in row 27, almost directly underneath the SDU.

I was unable to find anything about the Ukrainians from online news reports, but Brodsky had received some coverage in the Russian press. His wife, Elena, gave several interviews to local media. In one, she calmly indicated that her husband was still alive. "He'll be back," she told the Komsomolskaya Pravda, "and he will tell all." I started putting out feelers to find freelance investigators in Russia and Ukraine.

10.
DOPPELGANGER

On July 17 I was in my kitchen when the phone rang. It was a producer from CNN asking me if I could go on air to talk about the Malaysia Airlines 777 that had just gone down over Ukraine. I'd spent so much time thinking about Ukraine and MH370 that it took me a moment to realize that she was talking about a completely different airplane.

The details were still sketchy, but I gathered that in the late afternoon, Ukraine time, Malaysia Airlines Flight 17 had been flying from Amsterdam to Kuala Lumpur when it had exploded in midair. Initial reports suggested it might have been shot down by a surface-to-air missile while flying over territory held by Russia-backed rebels.

A Malaysia Airlines 777. Ukraine. Russia. I thought: They've done it again. I had no idea what the motive would be, any more than I knew what Russia's motive could be for taking MH370. But the similarities seemed too overwhelming to ignore. Boeing 777s are among the most reliable airplanes in the world; none had ever been lost mid-flight before. There were 15 Malaysia Airlines 777s at the start of 2014, out of some 18,000 registered aircraft in the world, and two had come to grief under mysterious circumstances in less than five months.

The statistical unlikelihood was off the charts, as I assumed everyone would recognize. I worried that my scoop would be stolen out from under me.

My fears proved groundless. On air at CNN, all the other aviation analysts agreed that of course the destruction of MH17 so soon after the loss of MH370 could only be a freak coincidence. What connection could there possibly be? When asked for my opinion, I said it was too early to draw any conclusions.

But my mind was whirring.

11.

OCTOBER 2014

Even while working on a hypothesis that ran counter to the official line, I had to stay on top of what government investigators were doing and why. My theory was just a possibility, after all, and it seemed far-fetched even to me. It would be safer for my reputation to publicly align myself with the consensus view that the Inmarsat data had not been altered and that the plane had gone south. So I followed search officials' announcements meticulously and remained active in internet discussions about the southern endpoint.

Now that the surface and underwater searches had both been called off, Australia began laying the groundwork for phase two, slated to commence during the southern spring. Ships would be dispatched to the 7th arc to survey a giant patch of the seabed using side-scan sonar. No search of this scale and difficulty had ever been attempted before. In the course of a normal investigation, side-scan sonar is used to locate wreckage whose general position has already been determined. It's a slow, small-scale process—like painting with a painter's brush instead of a roller. While a search plane can move hundreds of miles an hour and visually scan for many miles in either direction, a side-scan sonar moves at a walking pace and can only "see" a swath about a mile wide.

To have any hope of success, the search would have to focus on the area where the plane most likely went down. But where was that? As time went by, and the experts honed their understanding of the BFO signals, they kept running up against an intractable problem. It kept proving impossible to get the two Inmarsat data sets to line up.

The BTO data strongly implied that the plane had flown fast and straight. This made sense, as straight and fast are how planes are designed to fly. The BFO data, on the other hand, suggested that the plane either flew in circles for a while or took a curving path, in either case winding up further to the northeast. Despite investigators' best efforts, it proved hard to come up with a search area that matched both sets of data.

In an attempt to bring clarity to the issue, the ATSB called together an assembly of experts from a variety of disciplines. The aircraft's manufacturer, Boeing, and the maker of the SDU, Thales, brought proprietary knowledge of the 777 and its key systems. Inmarsat contributed its expertise in deciphering satellite dynamics and communications protocols. Aviation safety boards from the US, China, Malaysia, and Australia brought air-crash investigation know-how. And government bodies like

Australia's Defence Science and Technology Group (DSTG) contributed scientific expertise in specific domains.

While this was going on, PBS science journalist Miles O'Brien reached out to me and asked for help putting together a documentary for the PBS series "Nova." His production team had access to Inmarsat's scientists and engineers, including Mark Dickinson, vice president of satellite operations. We all got on a conference call and I asked the question I'd been dying to ask for months: how had they been able to determine that the data could not have been tampered with? Rather than offer technical reasons why a spoof would be impossible, Dickinson dismissed the idea as simply seeming too unlikely. For someone to have pulled off a spoof, he said, "whoever did that would have to have six month's worth of knowledge of what would happen, in essence have to know how the data would be used… there's nothing to show that evidence at all as far as I'm aware."

I took this to mean that a spoof would have been impossible because to pull it off the perpetrators would have to have been significantly smarter than the investigators. An inconceivable notion.

On October 8 the ATSB published their experts' latest findings. The paper defined a new search area hundreds of miles to the south of where they'd previously planned to look. This new search zone actually encompassed two separate but adjoining areas: one that made sense from the perspective of the BTO and how airliners actually fly, and another that better fit the BFO data. Together they delineated a curving strip of ocean 600 nautical miles long.

The logistical and technical challenges of searching this 23,000-square-mile area were enormous. Because it lay so far from land, crews would have to stay out for a month at a time, in a clime that mariners considered to be among the most inhospitable in the world. Here in the fabled "roaring forties" the waves at times reach 50 feet high.

When the weather was amenable, the ships would reel out torpedo-shaped devices called towfish on six-mile-long tethers. Scooting along 500 feet above the seabed, these emitted beams of high-frequency sound. The echoes they received were descrambled by computer to produce photograph-like images of what lay below. When the undersea terrain was too rugged, searchers deployed autonomous underwater vehicles, or AUVs, that darted more nimbly around obstructions.

In late October, the search vessel Fugro Discovery made its first pass towing side-scan sonar gear. It saw nothing, reached the end of its search zone, did a U-turn, and scanned a parallel swath. Over the next few months it steamed up and down parallel to the 7th arc, imaging the seabed in lawnmower strips, gradually working outward from the center of the search zone.

By now officials were confident that they'd got the numbers right, and believed that success would follow in short order. As lead Australian crash investigator Peter Foley told one reporter, "the 1988 Moet is chilling nicely."

12.

NOVEMBER 2014

Meanwhile, my investigative efforts in Ukraine and Russia were beginning to bear fruit.

A freelance researcher I hired in Irkutsk was able to interview one of Nikolai Brodsky's friends and three of his relatives. From their accounts she was able to assemble a rough outline of his life.

Born in 1971 in the Siberian city of Irkutsk, Brodsky moved with his family to the eastern province of Yakutia when he was eight. He then returned to Irkutsk when he was 16. He attended a local polytechnic but was a poor student. When he was 18, his girlfriend Nadia became pregnant, so they married and moved to Yakutia along with Brodsky's parents. The marriage was unhappy, and Nadia returned to Irkutsk alone. Brodsky followed, but the marriage ended soon after.

Brodsky subsequently moved to a small town further north where he worked for a timber-products company. For a time he attempted to continue his education via correspondence course, but the school eventually expelled him for poor performance. Then he hooked up with a future oligarch, Vitaly Mashchitsky, and his fortunes improved dramatically. While still in his 20s, Brodsky founded a wood-products company whose operations ultimately extended to three cities in Siberia and the Far East.

Brodsky's passion was technical scuba diving. He was proficient in the use of trimix gas breathing equipment, which allows dives to depths of 1,000 feet and is primarily used for commercial and military diving. Brodsky was active in a local scuba club and regularly made dives under the ice in nearby Lake Baikal. (A yearly club tradition is to brave subzero temperatures to hold an underwater party below the ice, complete with Christmas tree and a Santa who hands out gifts.) He was an instructor in the club, and at the time of his disappearance was on his way back from an 11-day club trip to Bali.

Brodsky's eldest son, 25-year-old Lyev, described his father as "a very strong and prepared person, both morally and physically... I've never known him to be afraid of anything." He said that Nikolai had never been in the military, having received an exemption from the draft due to flat feet. Lyev had no firsthand knowledge of his father's whereabouts between the age of 19 and 29, however, as Nikolai had left his mother soon after Lyev's birth and only reconnected with him later.

One of Brodsky's fellow dive club members also described Brodsky as fearless and exceptionally competent. When Brodsky first joined the club, the friend said, most of the members were ex-military who had learned to dive in the service. The first day

Brodsky showed up, he went in the water with two instructors and another first-time diver. Conditions were tricky, and the other beginner nearly panicked. Brodsky kept his cool. "Nick felt very comfortable and did not look like a novice diver," the friend said. Later, he got to know Brodsky as a man who "has a very good mentality, resistance to stress. In any situation it is collected, a sober assessment of what is happening can never be in vain to take risks." Brodsky was adept at rigging up whatever gear or amenity might be needed, out of whatever materials might be at hand. "We often joked about him that he is a hamster—in his car always find all the necessary and useful."

Brodsky most definitely enjoyed the challenge of diving under the ice, in poor visibility, at great depths, with special gases. But he did not enjoy diving in warm seas and tended to skip club trips to the tropics. "He took part almost in all dive-club activities except for long trips," his friend said. "His decision to go to Bali with club was pretty unexpected. He didn't love the warm water and this kind of activity."

Brodsky was on MH370 because he had decided to cut his vacation short by three days. According to early press accounts, this was because he had promised his wife that he would have dinner with her on International Women's Day, a kind of Soviet-era counterpart to Valentine's Day. His family, however, said that wasn't the reason, but rather that he had to make a business trip to Mongolia.

I had a much harder time finding out anything about the Ukrainians, Oleg Chustrak and Sergei

Deineka. The men had no presence on the web except for cursory, recently created profiles on Google Plus which contained little information beyond photographs.

Deineka's page listed his employer as an Odessa furniture company, Nika Mebel. The company sold upholstered furniture online but listed no physical address and only accepted cash payments. The website, which was registered in 2011 but only seemed to have been active since mid-2013, listed three phone numbers, all of which belonged to cell phones.

Nika Mebel's Google Plus page listed only two members: Oleg Chustrak and Sergei Deineka. But when a translator called Nika Mebel on my behalf, the man who answered said that neither man worked for the company, and that he knew nothing about them.

A second translator visited Chustrak's apartment for me and briefly spoke to his father, but the man didn't want to talk. He did say, however, that Oleg worked for Nika Mebel. A third translator then called the company and was told that not only did Oleg Chustrak once work there, his son still did. The translator then called Chustrak's son, who said he didn't know if he wanted to speak with us, and referred us to the family's lawyer. The lawyer refused to provide me with any information.

13.

DECEMBER 2014

Search officials were absolutely confident that they understood roughly where the plane had gone. But the ATSB had avoided laying out any theory about why it had gone there, insisting that its job was to find the plane, not to determine the cause.

The community of independent researchers, however, had long since arrived at a consensus. They identified MH370's captain, 53-year-old Zaharie Ahmad Shah, as the most likely culprit. A highly experienced pilot with 18,000 hours of flight time, Shah was the only person aboard the plane known to have sophisticated knowledge of the 777. What's more, only a minute had elapsed between Shah's calmly spoken final words to flight controllers —"Good Night, Malaysia 370"—and the switching off of the communications equipment. It was hard to imagine that passengers could have broken through a locked door and taken control of the airplane in such a short amount of time, all without the flight crew sending a mayday.

On the other hand, from a psychological perspective Shah seemed an unlikely candidate for mass-murder suicide. His family said he was a loving husband and father. His friends said he was a cheerful soul who loved to cook, fly model airplanes, and make balloon animals. His professional record was spotless. His YouTube channel consisted of home-improvement videos in which he demonstrated how to fix leaky windows and tweak an air conditioning system to save electricity. Though Muslim, he was no fundamentalist. He criticized terrorists, subscribed to Richard Dawkins' YouTube channel, and supported democratic reform in Malaysia. At the time of his disappearance he was looking forward to retiring to Australia.

With no slam-dunk evidence of Shah's guilt, all sorts of theories multiplied across the internet. The media, lacking the technical savvy to separate the wheat from the chaff and keen to serve up new angles on an immensely popular story, amplified each new idea no matter how outlandish. The result was a chronic fog of misinformation.

Some of the erroneous ideas were spread by apparently well-intentioned people who just didn't know what they didn't know. A Canadian pilot named Chris Goodfellow went viral with his theory that MH370 had suffered a fire that knocked out its communications gear and had diverted from its planned route in order to attempt an emergency landing. Keith Ledgerwood, another recreational pilot, made waves with his theory that hijackers had taken MH370 and ducked into the radar shadow of another airliner heading for the Middle East. Others felt certain that MH370 had been taken over by hackers and shot down by the United States to prevent the plane from being used in a 9/11-style attack on Diego Garcia, a military base on an atoll in the center of the Indian Ocean. Each of these theories received a flurry of attention in the media, but none fit the evidence.

In the fringes of social media the fog lay even thicker. Everywhere the case was being discussed online, the conversation was dominated by cranks peddling fever-dream theories. As the proprietor of the most active web site, I found myself constantly beset. No matter how much time others spent pointing out the logical flaws, these people would keep at it, needling and prodding the discussion back around to their pet theories. One was convinced that the plane had been hit by lightning and then floated in the South China Sea for seven hours, transmitting to the satellite on battery power. When I kicked him off the site he came back under aliases. I wound up banning anyone who used the word "lightning." At first I assumed that people like this were all garden-variety cranks, obsessives who'd gotten sucked into a mental feedback loop. In time, though, I began to wonder if their motivation was more malicious.

Eventually, confusion became the case's defining characteristic. The words "MH370" and "conspiracy theory" became so closely linked that whenever I told anyone that I was working on the story, they'd winkingly ask, "So do you think a UFO took it?"

I understood the ribbing. I'd gone deep down the rabbit hole, and I knew it. The CNN checks by now were a distant memory, and I was spending vast amounts of time on an obsession that earned me not a cent. Worse than that, I was forking out my own money for translators and researchers. I knew I needed to move on and find work that would pay. But all I could think about was that damned plane.

On December 1, 2014, I published the first installment of a six-part blog post laying out my hypothesis that MH370's satellite communication system had been hacked and the plane flown north to Russia. I explained my suspicions concerning Brodsky, Chustrak, and Deineka, and argued that since the missile that took down MH17 could only have been fired by the order senior echelons, the Kremlin must have been responsible for the destruction of both Malaysia Airlines 777s. In the new year, I collected the posts into an e-book called *The Plane that Wasn't There*, which Amazon picked up as a Kindle Single. I then wrote a feature article for *New York* magazine that ran under headline: "How Crazy Am I to Think I Actually Know Where That Malaysia Airlines Plane Is?"

The e-book and the magazine article caused a stir. As the anniversary of the disappearance approached, I was invited onto Fox News, MSNBC and CNN to talk about my research. Not everyone bought my theory. CNN host Richard Quest pronounced it preposterous. Russian network RT declared that I suffered from "Putin Derangement Syndrome."

I'd made an extremely public gamble, and it caused me no end of anxiety. Any day now, the ATSB's search team could find the plane and prove me wrong. But I felt an obligation to call the case the way I saw it. It would be embarrassing to be mistaken, but how much worse if it turned out I'd been right and hadn't said anything?

Whenever the self-doubt grew too strong, I'd think of the timing of the disappearance five seconds after IGARI, the aggressiveness of the U-turn, the high speed flight to the west, and the SDU re-boot. Whoever did this was aggressive and sophisticated. Their aim clearly seemed to be to outfox any pursuers. If evasion was their goal at the beginning of the flight, it seemed reasonable to presume that it was their goal throughout.

PART 2
The Search

14.

APRIL 2015

By April 2015 the search ships had scoured 60 percent of the planned search area, a swathe more than 500 nautical miles long and 25 miles wide. The laws of probability dictated that the further they moved away from the 7th arc, the less likely they'd find something in any given sweep. While the ATSB maintained an external veneer of confidence, internally doubts were starting to grow that the search might not be successful after all.

If that turned out to be the case, the question would be: Where else could the plane have gone?

As officials saw it, there were two possibilities. The first was that the investigators had misidentified the range of possible endpoints along the 7th arc where the plane could have gone. Perhaps it had flown further to the southwest or northeast. But ATSB investigators felt that either scenario was unlikely. To reach a point further to the southwest, the plane would have had to have flown very fast, and in so doing would have burned more fuel than it carried. To have flown further to the northeast, on the other hand, the plane would have to have flown slower than normal. To do that in a way that matched the ping rings would require a curving path. Planes don't fly that way on any standard autopilot settings.

There is another way that MH370 might have ended up outside the search area. It could have flown on further after the final transmission than investigators originally considered likely.

As you'll recall, we found out back in June of 2014 that the SDU had turned off when the plane first vanished, then came back online at 18:25. As a result, the data that Inmarsat recorded during that first ping was long and complex, involving a back-and-forth exchange of data required to establish a logon. The five pings that followed were shorter and simpler, part of a regular check-in routine that Inmarsat's network carries out whenever a user is inactive for an hour.

The sixth and penultimate automatic exchange took place at 0:11. Then something happened. When MH370's SDU contacted Inmarsat eight minutes later, at 0:19, it was requesting a log-on just it had at 18:25. Once again, evidently, the SDU had lost power and then been turned back on.

Investigators had no idea why the SDU rebooted the first time, at 18:25, but they thought they understood why it rebooted at 0:19. At that point the plane was nearly eight hours into what had been scheduled as a six-and-a-half-hour flight. The fuel tanks, then, must have been very close to empty. Once the engines ran out of fuel the generators would have cut out. The entire aircraft would have lost electrical power, including the SDU. At that point an emergency generator called the Alternate Power Unit would have automatically kicked in and restored power to select critical systems. After a minute-long power-up process the SDU would have re-established contact with Inmarsat. Without engine power to provide thrust, however, the plane would have been steadily losing speed and altitude en route to an inevitable crash.

The final BFO values offered a clue as to how fast the plane was descending during its final moments. The first, at 0:19:29, signified a vertical speed of between 4,000 and 14,000 feet per minute —a velocity toward the ground of 45 to 160 mph. Eight seconds later it was plummeting even faster, between 15,000 and 25,000 feet per minute, or 170 to 284 miles per hour. That change is equivalent to an acceleration of two-thirds of what the plane would experience freefalling in a vacuum. Given that the aircraft achieved this without engine thrust, it must have been pointing nearly straight down. For this to be the case, either someone had to have pushed the nose down in a deliberate dive, or there was no one at the controls and the plane had sloughed off into a spiral dive on its own. Either way, when the ATSB conducted simulations in which the plane went into a dive like this, it always hit the ocean within 15 nautical miles.

In other words, the plane should already have been found within the defined search area.

What to do? The investigators had to make a decision. The southern winter was drawing near. Soon high seas and fierce winds would make deploying the towfish too difficult and dangerous. The search would have to be suspended until the southern spring.

On April 16, 2014, officials from Malaysia, Australia, and China met in Kuala Lumpur to hammer out a plan. In the end, they decided that simply giving up was not a politically viable option. They issued a communiqué announcing that they were doubling the search area to 46,000 square miles. The newly defined search area stretched a bit further along the 7th arc and was nearly twice as wide. The officials stated that if the plane weren't found in this newly expanded area, the search would be called off for good.

But then the story took yet another hard left turn.

15.

JULY 2015

At 8.30am on July 29, 2015, on the northeastern shore of Réunion Island, a French territory in the western Indian Ocean, a cleanup crew was working its way along a stretch of pebbly beach when a worker named Johnny Begue spotted an unfamiliar-looking object at the edge of the surf. Roughly rectangular and about six feet long, it somewhat resembled a stubby airplane wing encrusted with marine life. Intrigued, the men lifted the object and carried it higher up the shore.

Soon gendarmes were on the scene, along with local news photographers. The officers put the piece into the back of a Land Rover. Within days it had been packed up, loaded onto an airplane, and flown to France.

News of the find caused a sensation. From photographs circulating on the web, the piece was quickly identified as a flaperon, a part of the wing's trailing edge. The flaperon's function combines those of a flap, which droop down to allow a plane to fly more slowly on descent to landing, with those of an aileron, which are raised or lowered to cause a plane to turn. Specifically, this flaperon was identified as coming from the right wing of a Boeing 777. Since the only 777 ever lost at sea was MH370, investigators now had physical evidence to back up what the math had been telling them: the plane had gone into the southern Indian Ocean.

France could have turned the flaperon it over to the Malaysians, but instead decided to keep it and launch their own investigation. It was delivered into the care of the Direction Générale de l'Armement (DGA), France's weapons development and procurement agency. At a laboratory in Toulouse, investigators rooted around inside the flaperon with an endoscopic probe and found serial numbers that matched records kept by the manufacturer in Spain. Now there was no doubt that the first piece of MH370 had been found.

Up until this point, the spoof scenario had slowly been gaining adherents among journalists and independent researchers. But for many the discovery of debris instantly rendered it a dead letter. The first question everyone had for me now was, "So I guess you were wrong, huh?"

I wasn't so sure. The idea that someone might falsify physical evidence in order to throw investigators off the scent struck many as conspiracy-theory craziness. But I didn't see it that way. To me it seemed that if MH370 had been hijacked via a hack, then planting debris would be basic tradecraft. Indeed, after the Soviets accidentally shot down Korean Airlines Flight 007 over the Sea of Japan in 1983, they reportedly planted false acoustic pingers on the seabed to thwart U.S. search efforts.

For me, the most important thing to investigate was whether anything about the debris ruled in, or ruled out, the possibility that it had been planted. The French were keeping their investigation under tight wraps, but some intriguing tidbits leaked out. According to a report in the French website LaDepeche.fr, scientists who examined the flaperon determined that it had not floated at the surface but had drifted entre deux eaux—a phrase which literally translates to "between two waters," but here means fully immersed, at a depth of several meters. This was puzzling. Inanimate objects cannot float neutrally buoyant underwater.

From personal experience as a scuba diver, I knew that when you're underwater, you're always either more or less buoyant than the surrounding water. By adjusting your weights and the volume of air in your buoyancy control device, you can come close to neutral and hover almost motionless, but every time you breathe in you will start to rise a little bit, and every time you breathe out you will start to sink. If you see a scuba diver suspended motionless over a coral reef, what they're really doing is subtly rising and falling.

An inert object cannot adjust its buoyancy and will either sink or rise. "It is very hard to build something that will float slightly below the surface," David Griffin, an oceanographer with the Commonwealth Scientific and Industrial Research Organisation (CSIRO), wrote me in an email. "The probability that an aircraft part does this is miniscule. The only way it can do this is if some of the object breaks the surface. If it does not break the surface AT ALL it must sink."

I had no idea how long it would take the French to release a report on their findings, but I realized that I might be able to check the "entre deux eaux" assertion on my own. Using Google and Bing image search, I tracked down photographs of the flaperon taken at every angle by journalists who were on hand immediately after the piece was discovered. I saw barnacles growing on every surface.

I reached out to marine biologists who study these animals and learned that the specimens, commonly known as goose barnacles, belonged to a species called Lepas anatifera. These barnacles live exclusively on debris floating in the open ocean. Their larvae spend the early part of their lives swimming freely, then find an object on which to settle. In general, Lepas barnacles like to spread out and prefer the shade. They generally avoid territory close to the waterline, where the rising and falling waves periodically expose them to the air. "The uppermost centimeters of water are normally a quite harsh environment," Hans-Georg Herbig of the Institut für Geologie und Mineralogie in Cologne, Germany, told me in an email. Exposed to sun and rain, they experience drastic changes in temperature and salinity as well as intense UV radiation.

Given the right environment, though, Lepas barnacles are notoriously fast-growing. The floating debris on which they have evolved to live is most often organic, and eventually will break apart and sink, so time is of the essence. Whereas a species of goose barnacle that lives on rocks might take five years to reach sexual maturity, Lepas can do it in mere weeks. And they settle quickly on any material that winds up in the ocean.

"I've picked a paper bag out of the Pacific that had barnacle larvae on it," said Cynthia Venn, a professor of oceanography and geology at Bloomsburg University in Pennsylvania. As a result, Lepas-colonized flotsam can become extremely crowded in short order.

"Goose barnacles grow spectacularly fast," Charles Griffiths, an emeritus professor of marine biology at the University of Cape Town, told me via email. "I have seen very large barnacles (as long as my finger) growing on a cable known to have only been in the water for 6 weeks."

It might be possible, I realized, to infer how long the flaperon had been in the water from the size of its barnacles. But how big were they, exactly?

At first I was stumped. The flaperon was broken and jagged, so there was nothing of known size that I could gauge the shells against. Then as I dug through images online I came upon a photograph of gendarmes loading the flaperon into the back of a Land Rover. I found a diagram with the exact dimensions of this particular Land Rover model and used it to determine the dimensions of the flaperon, and by extension the dimensions of the Lepas shells. I calculated the shells on the biggest ones to be approximately 2.3 cm long.

Next I found a paper by a Japanese researcher named Yoichi Yusa who had studied the growth rate of a related Lepas species, Lepas anserifera. Using his data I calculated that it would take about 109 days, or four months, for Lepas to grow to this size. I also emailed Yusa photographs of the flaperon and asked him to estimate how long they'd been growing, and he answered: "I would guess that they had been there for a short time (between 2 weeks and a few months)."

Cynthia Venn's seat-of-the-pants estimate was "less than six months."

Recall that Lepas larvae are widespread throughout the ocean and aggressively colonize any available surface. If the flaperon had been in the water from March 8, 2014 to July 31, 2015, we would expect to find Lepas that were more than a year old.

So the barnacles weren't the right age for an object that had been in the water for 15 months, and the way they were distributed implied a violation of the laws of buoyancy. Together, these observations suggested that the piece might have come to its final condition and location through something other than natural means.

16.
NOVEMBER 2015

If search officials shared my concerns, they weren't letting on. Instead, the first piece of verified debris seemed to have reinvigorated their confidence that the plane was in the southern Indian Ocean. And they were increasingly confident in their math. "The experts are telling us that there is a 97 percent possibility that it is in that area," Australian Deputy Prime Minister Warren Truss told the *Wall Street Journal*.

Behind the scenes a team of experts had quietly been developing new analytical tools to more precisely determine where the plane had gone. The effort was led by Dr. Neil Gordon, a scientist at Australia's Defense Science & Technology Group (DSTG). Gordon's team devised a mathematical approach based on Bayes' theorem, a tool for gauging the probability of possible outcomes based on a set of initial parameters. They revealed the details of their work on November 30, 2015 in a paper entitled "Bayesian Methods in the Search for

MH370."

This approach was based entirely on BTO values —the timing data. The experts had come to realize that the BFO values—the frequency data—were shot through with too much uncertainty to add meaningfully to an understanding of the plane's path.

It involved generating a huge number of random routes flown at different speeds with different numbers of turns and testing them to see which best fit the observed BTO data. It turned out that routes with high speed and no turns (or a few very small turns) fit the BTO data well, while most of those with more significant turns or slower speed did not.

The DSTG plotted the endpoints along the 7th arc. The result was a "heat map" representing the relative probability of the plane's having ended up in any given location. It looked like a diffuse, elongated blob. To make sure their technique was valid, the scientists performed the same calculations on other flights in which they had both BTO data and the actual route flown. It checked out.

Based on their calculations, the DSTG defined a search area that stretched about 400 miles along the 7th arc, from latitude 35° south to latitude 39° south —a more compact area than the previously defined one. The results only reinforced investigators' conviction that they'd been searching the right stretch of seabed all along.

The paper attracted widespread attention. But there was a detail buried within that was uniquely interesting to me. Page 85 of the report contains a Google Earth screenshot of the eastern hemisphere overlaid by the routes in the DSTG's probability calculation. The routes all begin with a flight path running up the Malacca Strait. Then they fork into two subsets.

Recall that routes generated from BTO data alone are inherently ambiguous, in that they create an equally valid mirror image. The BFO data is then used to decide which one is correct. The caption for this image, however, explained that the sets of paths were made "using only BTO measurement weighting (i.e. not using BFO measurements)." On display, in other words, were both the route and its mirror.

One subset takes a hard left around the western tip of Sumatra and plunges into the remote Indian Ocean. This is the famous southern route seen in countless TV and newspaper graphics. The other

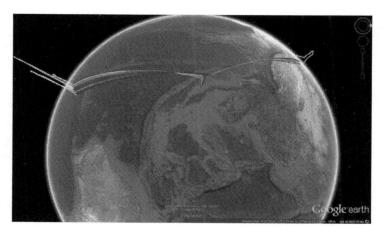

subset takes a slight turn to the right, passes over the Andaman Islands and crosses the Indian coast near Calcutta. It then tops the ridge of the Himalayas in western Nepal and skirts the border between India and China before flying over Kyrgyzstan and into

Kazakhstan.

The official assumption was that the BFO data was valid, and the plane had flown one of the subset of routes that turned south, and the subset that turned north were the spurious mirror images. If my suspicions were correct, however, and the BFO data had been tampered with, then officials had got it exactly backwards. The plane's actual route lay to the north, and the southern routes were the mirror ones.

In effect, the DSTG had revealed where the plane went if the Inmarsat data had been spoofed.

17.
RADAR

For as long as searchers have been aware of the existence of the Inmarsat data, there has always been one particularly compelling reason to suspect that the plane went south rather than north. If it had gone north, it would have passed through the air-defense radars of multiple countries, including the two most populous on Earth. Yet no one had reported seeing it.

It would seem common sense to assume that most nation's militaries routinely monitor their airspace. That turns out not to be the case, however. Military radar is expensive to build and requires a lot of electricity and manpower to operate. Unless there is a valuable target to defend, and missiles and planes capable of defending it, running a radar station 24/7 isn't worth the cost. So in most parts of the world coverage is like Swiss Cheese in reverse: the gaps far outnumber the areas under surveillance.

"During the Cold War, we got used to the concept that the radar is constantly on and jets are scrambled if anything unexpected is seen," Tim Huxley, executive director of the International Institute of Strategic Studies in Asia, told the Wall Street Journal in 2014. "We sort of expect that to be the normal response, but that doesn't necessarily translate into comprehensive coverage in other parts of the world."

If MH370 did fly north, what kind of radar environment would it have passed through?

Let's start with the beginning of the route. Half an hour after leaving the Malacca Strait, according to the DSTG's calculations, the plane would have passed over the Andaman Islands. The archipelago belongs to India, which maintains a radar station there. But the radar is only turned on when a crisis is looming, which wasn't the case on March 8. "We operate on an 'as required' basis," the chief of staff of India's Andamans and Nicobar Command told Reuters.

Next, the plane would have crossed the coast of mainland India west of Calcutta and passed almost directly over the air force base at Kalaikunda. The Russian-built Sukhoi Su-30 fighters stationed there are guided by the nearby radar installation at Salua. But if the Andaman radar was inactive, Salua likely was as well, since both facilities are geared toward defence of the same area. "Kalaikunda... has been a bridge with the Andamans," an official told the Times of India in 2011. "The role of the base will grow and aircraft based here will play a vital role in patrolling the skies over the Andamans and the Bay of Bengal."

The Indian military is notoriously underfunded

and poorly equipped, so it's not surprising that it focuses its assets on the one region where it faces and ongoing threat: its border with Pakistan, 1,000 miles to the northwest. Relations between the countries have been tense since they achieved independence from Britain in 1947. In 1971 a surprise attack by Pakistani jets against Indian air bases and radar stations precipitated a 13-day war in which more than 10,000 soldiers died. Numerous unresolved territorial claims continue to foment distrust. On February 27, 2019, Pakistan shot down an Indian MiG-21 fighter that had crossed into its airspace.

Even when tensions are not running high, India routinely intercepts any planes that happen to cross into its airspace from Pakistan without adhering to correct air-traffic procedure. It is less vigilant about the Bay of Bengal. "India has an exceptionally large area to cover, a massive airspace and maritime space," Huxley told the Wall Street Journal. "Looking toward the south, they wouldn't have so much reason to expect adversary aircraft."

Continuing northward, MH370 would have crossed into Nepalese airspace. Nepal is a small, poor country with no air force or air defense radar.

Passing west of Kathmandu, the plane would have traversed the spine of the Himalayas and entered Chinese airspace. For the next two hours it would have hewn to the far western edges of Tibet and Xinjiang, China's two westernmost provinces.

The region is something of an aeronautical desert. If you look at a flight-tracking web site you'll see steady streams of traffic flowing to the north, south, east, and west, but a void here. The reason most flights avoid the area is that if they suffer accidental depressurization there they won't be able to descend to the mandated altitude of 10,000 feet. Much of the Tibetan plateau lies above 15,000 feet in elevation, so that even on the ground crew members acclimatized to sea level would need supplemental oxygen. There is one route across far western China that Lufthansa uses to connect Frankfurt and Hong Kong, but it can only be flown by specially trained crews in specially equipped aircraft.

Due to the lack of air traffic, there is no radar coverage in this part of China. Planes flying the route are required to stay in touch with air traffic control via satellite datalink. Then, once the flight clears the plateau and passes over more populated, lower-lying areas in the eastern part of the country, air traffic control become normal again: "As soon was we are out of this area we are on radar," says Lufthansa pilot Peter Klant, who has flown the route extensively.

The same conditions that discourage civilian aviation also make the region inhospitable for military aircraft and air defense. Its huge size, remoteness, high altitude, and fierce weather make it difficult to defend; the fact that it is largely empty further means there's little to attack anyway. The region remains a backwater of Chinese strategic air defence.

"The real threats that China faces are east, along the coast," says Timothy R. Heath, a senior defense research analyst at the RAND corporation who studies Chinese military aviation. "They have air defenses down south, facing Taiwan and Vietnam, and up near the Korean peninsula, which makes sense because all of those are countries with aircraft and missiles that can harm China. The Indian border is primarily a ground infantry situation, due to the terrain— it's hard for aircraft to locate and target anything."

Three Chinese airbases lie on or near MH370's route.

The first, Ngari Gunsa, is a remote 15,000-foot airstrip laid out along a broad, barren valley in the Gandise range. Its altitude of 14,000 feet makes it the fourth-highest altitude airport in the world. Intended for both military and civilian use, its construction was begun in 2007 and completed in 2010. But fighter deployment since then has been infrequent. According to a 2017 article in Indian Defence Review, since 2010 the Chinese air force has been deploying jets only "twice every year for two-week deployment periods."

About 125 miles after Ngari Gunsa the plane would have crossed from Tibet into Xinjiang. Its path would have taken it about 100 miles west of Hotan, also known as Hetian, an ancient silk road town on the southwestern edge of the Taklamakan Desert. Hetian appears to have been used as a temporary staging area for fighter planes. There are no military aircraft visible in the Google Earth satellite image of the site taken in February, 2013; in September of that year 26 jets and two helicopters can be seen. The following month the ramp is again bare. Then in October, 2014, 16 military jets are visible.

This kind of temporary staging is "what I'd expect," says Heath. "Some of these environments are really hard on the equipment. They'll move the air defence out there for a while, do some exercises, and then they'll pull it back."

Just before it left Chinese airspace, MH370 would have passed almost directly over the oasis city of Kashgar, also known as Kashi. Google Earth imagery shows that in March of 2014 construction had begun on a new ramp area at the eastern end of the city's commercial airport. This would ultimately become the home of a fighter squadron. But the first planes wouldn't arrive for another three years.

Interestingly, in the wake of MH370's disappearance, China stepped up its overall air defense capabilities in the region, in particular flying "confrontation drills" and "paying much attention to the training of air battle at night," according to a 2017 story in Delhi Defence Review. In 2015, the Chinese air force deployed its most advanced anti-aircraft missile system, the HQ-9, to Hotan. "It's kind of odd that they would even have HQ-9s out in Xinjiang," Heath says. "What's the threat?"

Six hours after diverting from its planned route, MH370 would have been nearing the border of the former Soviet Union. If the hijacking had been commanded by the Kremlin, then the perpetrators would now be home safe. Directly ahead would be the first of the former Soviet states, Kyrgyzstan. Twenty minutes later, the Russian airbase at Kant would lie abeam the starboard wing. Ahead would stretch the expanse of Kazakhstan's Betpak-Dala desert. And off to the left, a half-hour's flying distance away, would lie the Baikonur Cosmodrome.

18.

FEBRUARY 2016

If there was one piece of debris, there must have been a lot more out there somewhere. Yet month after month went by without any further discoveries. Then, on February 28, 2016, I received an email from an independent researcher named Blaine Alan Gibson.

> Dear Jeff
> Please read my post in *The Longest Journey* [a members-only Facebook discussion group] about the debris my friend and I found in Mozambique. I will be attending the two year commemoration in Kuala Lumpur March 6. I still hope you and I can meet in person soon to discuss MH 370. I am increasingly doubtful about the validity of the Inmarsat data and its interpretation.
> Best wishes,
> Blaine Gibson

I'd first become aware of Gibson the previous June. Another MH370 researcher who went by the handle Nihonmama had posted a comment on my web page naming Gibson as a retired Seattle lawyer on a self-financed trip around the Indian Ocean region looking for clues about the missing plane. Gibson had just been on a trip to the remote island of Kudahuvadhoo in the Maldives, Nihonmama said, where villagers reportedly had seen a plane in red-and-blue livery fly low overhead the morning after MH370's disappearance.

This was one of those "fog" stories which serious researchers had always ignored. Eyewitness testimony is notoriously unreliable, and there was no way the Inmarsat data was compatible with the plane's appearance over Maldives. But Gibson was convinced that the villagers really had seen MH370, perhaps as it headed toward a suicide mission at Diego Garcia. To me, this idea marked him instantly as a crank.

Then in September, Gibson had reported on Facebook that he'd visited Réunion and hunted down Johnny Begue to learn more about the discovery of the flaperon. This was more interesting to me, so I reached out to him and we exchanged a few messages. In one-on-one exchanges he struck me as affable, coherent, and concise, as well as a competent speller, which means a lot when you're dealing with people on the internet.

Two months later Gibson popped up again. He'd posted on Facebook about a shadowy meeting that supposedly took place in a remote corner of Vietnam two months before MH370 disappeared. In his account, an unidentified arms broker had produced a mysterious Soviet chemical warfare agent, a clear liquid in a glass-lined bottle, and melted a plastic water bottle down to a puddle with a single drop. The locals supposedly had dubbed the stuff "water dissolves metal." Now Gibson was proposing that MH370's hijackers had tried to use it to break through the cockpit door but had accidentally caused the hull to depressurize, leading to a hypoxic ghost flight to oblivion.

I mentally re-filed him in the lunatic fringe.

Nevertheless, when I got his February email about debris in Mozambique, I took it seriously enough to click through. I found pictures of a triangular slab of composite with a honeycomb interior, and a note saying that Gibson had found the piece the previous day on a sand bar near the town of Vilankulo. The piece bore the words "No Step."

Gibson shared his information with some members of the Independent Group, but made everyone swear to secrecy, for reasons that weren't clear to me. Within a few days the find was made public anyway. Malaysia's transport minister, Liow Tiong Lai, tweeted that there was a "high possibility debris found in Mozambique belongs to a B777."

Overnight, a man who'd lurked on the farthest fringes of the story became a worldwide celebrity. Television networks scrambled to interview him. Due our past association, he graciously granted me one of the first interviews, and I talked to him over the phone for 30 minutes for New York magazine. Among the surprising details he revealed was that he'd had the idea to go to Vilankulo after asking

Charitha Pattiaratchi, an Australian oceanographer who was working with the ATSB, where the highest probability search area would be. Pattiaratchi had recommended the coast of Mozambique.

Gibson had gone out to a sandbar with local boatmen and found "No Step" after only 20 minutes —an incredible stroke of luck.

The publicity surrounding Gibson's find triggered a wave of debris-reporting. On March 11, a South African teenager named Liam Lötter told local reporters that he'd found something similar on a beach near the resort town of Xai Xai in southern Mozambique in December. Only after he'd seen Gibson's story did he have any idea what it could be. Approximately a meter long, it carried the stencilled code "676EB," which identified it as a right-hand outboard flap faring from a Boeing 777. Two weeks later, a man strolling on a beach in Mossel Bay in South Africa found a piece of an engine cowling, and a week after that a vacationing couple on Rodrigues Island in Mauritius found a chunk of an interior cabin panel.

This sudden wave of debris was a remarkable turn of events. Now, many felt, there was no doubt that the plane had flown into the southern Indian Ocean.

But as I examined photographs of the newly discovered debris, something struck me as odd. Most of the pieces were remarkably clean. When man-made material is immersed in an oceanic ecosystem, any number of plant, animal, and microbial species will begin to settle and grow upon its surface, a process known as "marine biofouling" because historically the process has attracted the most attention as a nuisance to mariners. "The first thing that settles is microalgae, which looks like a slimy brown scummy scuzz," says Cathryn Clarke Murray, a marine biologist who studies floating debris at the North Pacific Marine Science Organization. Out in the open ocean, microalgae is followed by bryozoans —moss-like filter feeders—and goose barnacles of the genus Lepas.

Given the great size of the Earth's oceans, and the relatively slow speed at which objects drift (on the order of dozens of miles per day), objects encountered on the open sea have plenty of time to become colonized by these species. During a survey of debris in the Pacific, marine biologist Miriam Goldstein of the Scripps Institution of Oceanography collected 242 objects and found that all had organisms growing on them, except for two that were one square inch in size. University of Florida biologist Mike Gil conducted a similar survey in the eastern Pacific and "didn't find any clean debris, bottle cap size and larger."

The mix of species present on an object can yield clues about how it has drifted, a process that renowned invertebrate biologist James Carlton, director of the Williams-Mystic Maritime Studies Program in Mystic, Connecticut, has labeled "bioforensics." In his study of marine debris, including fishing boats, that washed out to sea during the Japanese tsunami of 2011, Carlton found that he could track how they traveled across the ocean using two species of bryozoans. "One's cold water, one's warm water," Carlton says. "When I get a boat that lands in Washington or Oregon and has the warm-water bryozoan, it tells me that it went well south before turning north." Similarly, Carlton has been able to identify debris that traveled south along the coast of Japan before crossing the Pacific by the presence of sea life endemic to that area.

Yet all the pieces that Gibson turned up, and most of the others, looked—at least in photographs, to the naked eye—to be free of marine life. The biologists I spoke to said that if an object is washed ashore, it can become dried out and get picked clean by scavenging animals so that little evidence of fouling remains. But "No Step" had been found on a tidal shoal, and others had been found shortly after they washed ashore. They just shouldn't have been that clean.

19.

MAY 2016

Out of the clear blue sky, a major break landed in my lap. A reader who said he was connected to some of the Chinese next-of-kin forwarded me what looked like cellphone pictures taken of an unreleased French document, "Rapport d'étude Dérive à rebours de flaperon" ("Flaperon Reverse Drift Study Report"), dated February 8, 2016.

The author, Pierre Daniel, was the head of the marine drift modeling unit at France's meteorological authority. He had been brought into the MH370 investigation to conduct a reverse-drift analysis. Using historical current and wind data, French investigators hoped to "rewind the tape" on drift simulations to generate a probability map showing where the piece most likely started out.

The reverse drift calculations would only work, however, if Daniel had a key parameter to plug in: the flaperon's windage. In other words, when it was floating in the ocean, how far above the water's surface did it stick up? If it was flush with the surface, the wind would hardly have made a difference, but if it floated high in the water, then the force of the wind would have changed its path considerably.

Scientists at the DGA put the flaperon in a large tank of water and found that it floated high. This

meant that the wind would indeed have played a large role in the path that the flaperon would have taken. Daniel's resulting calculations found that the flaperon could have started its drift from anywhere within a large swath of the Indian Ocean, starting at Cape Leeuwin in Australia and stretching southwestward. This area included the current seabed search zone.

There was a catch, however. When the French investigators took a careful look at the flaperon, they noticed the same thing that I had: The whole flaperon was covered in Lepas barnacles.

"The presence of crustaceans of the genus Lepas on two sides of the flaperon suggests... a piece that was totally immersed," the report concluded.

This, at last, was confirmation of the "entre deux eaux" claim.

The French scientists were baffled as to how reconcile these two seemingly irreconcilable facts. Throwing up their hands, they resigned themselves to performing two separate simulation runs. They found that, if the flaperon floated as the tank tests suggested, it could have come from the current search area. But if was fully submerged, as the Lepas distribution suggested, it most likely started out in the tropics northwest of Australia, 1,000 miles or more from the search zone.

20.

JUNE 2016

So much about about the debris just didn't make sense.

The high-speed impact of a 777 with the ocean surface would create a vast amount of floating debris. But that material would quickly disperse, as the swirls and eddies of the ocean currents pulled it in random directions. According to an animation produced by David Griffin's team at CSIRO, crash debris that started at the presumed impact zone, near 35° south, would by mid-2016 stretch from Cape Horn to Western Australia and as far north as the Horn of Africa, an area of some 10 million square miles. Much of it would have sunk; much of it would still be circulating in the eddies and gyres of the central ocean; the pieces that came ashore would be dispersed across 10,000 miles of coastline. Anyone beachcombing for MH370 debris would find better odds playing Powerball.

That didn't stop people from trying, of course. People all around the world were fascinated by

MH370. In South Africa and Australia, in particular, many beachgoers were on the lookout for debris.

Each year, a nonprofit organization called the Tangaroa Blue Foundation holds an event called the Western Australia Beach Cleanup. Some 1500 volunteers comb 130 beaches up and down the western coast collecting plastic rubbish and other debris, well aware that they might stumble upon evidence that could help solve history's most puzzling aviation mystery. "When [MH370] first happened, and they said where they thought it went down, I said to myself, 'Oh crap,'" because I knew this is where it would come," event organizer Renee Mouritz told me. With those drift patterns in mind, the organization set up an informal protocol to pass along reports of any suspected MH370 debris. But so far, Mouritz says, "nobody has fed anything back to us."

A similar organization conducts beach cleanups in South Africa. Each year the 20,000 participants are given a flyer reminding them to keep an eye out for potential pieces of aircraft debris. No one has yet found anything. Likewise, I talked to boatmen and fishing guides who spend most of their time in the waters of the western Indian Ocean, and they told me they've spotted nothing despite keeping a constant vigil.

So the many, many people who have deliberately looked for debris over the years have never found any—except one man. Over and over—a dozen times or more. That man is Blaine Alan Gibson.

After receiving a whirlwind of press attention for his first find, Gibson traveled to Ile Ste Marie,

Madagascar, in June accompanied by a crew from France 2 TV. There, according to the online publication Seattle Met:

> They rode quads along the beach, and at the north end he signaled for the party to stop. The camera crew had a good reason to follow him: He is, to this day, still the only person to find a piece of Flight 370 while actually looking for it. And he'd done enough research to have a good idea where he might find more. But come on, it was still a one-in-a-million find. There's no way he'd actually uncover another.
>
> Right?
>
> With the cameras trained on him, Gibson dismounted and started walking. And as he got closer to the object that had caught his eye, he could see that it was gray fiberglass. It was almost a clone of No Step. Later, he found a handful of other pieces, one of which looked exactly like the housing for a seat-back TV monitor. He couldn't be sure, but he had a pretty good idea they came from Flight 370.

If it's remarkable to find a piece of MH370 with TV cameras rolling, imagine doing it twice.

Later that year Gibson was back on Ile Ste Marie, this time with a delegation of MH370 family members and a documentary crew. On the morning of December 8, the group split up and spent the day combing separate areas. The camera crew followed Blaine. Having driven along one stretch of shore on an ATV and found nothing, he turned around and was making his way back when he came upon a piece of debris at the edge of the wet sand. A wave had evidently deposited it within the few minutes since he had passed. "Appears to be Malaysia 370 interior cabin debris," he declared.

And that wasn't all. Gibson found yet another piece under extraordinary circumstances. In a seaside village on mainland Madagascar he happened to spot a nine-year-old girl using a scrap of MH370 debris to fan a kitchen fire. "It was light and it was solid and it was part of the plane," Gibson told The Guardian. "When I put the word out around the village, another guy turned up with another piece he had been using as a washing board for clothes."

I found it implausible that one might happen upon someone fanning a fire with a flat object that just happened to be a piece of MH370. I became even more suspicious after I found that Gibson had given a different account of how he'd collected the piece in a posting to a closed Facebook group: "We combed the beach ourselves and found one piece of aircraft debris, a hexagonal rubber torque coupling seal... We showed pictures of debris to local people and asked if they had found any, and over the next two days different people brought us the remaining three pieces."

No mention of the girl. Had he changed his story, or merely simplified it? And if the former, was he motivated simply by the desire to tell an interesting story, or by something darker?

21.

SEPTEMBER 2016

As 2016 rolled on, the ships of the search flotilla continued to sail up and down the southern ocean, battling foul weather, seasickness, and monotony. There was a rare moment of excitement when their side scan sonar revealed the tell-tale oval-shaped debris field of a smashed vessel, but when the robot sub went down to take a closer look, it found a long-forgotten merchant ship.

Nevertheless, Australian officials continued to voice confidence that the seabed search would ultimately prove successful. On the second anniversary of the disappearance, ATSB head Martin Dolan told the Guardian that MH370 would be located before the end of the year. "It's as likely on the last day [of the search] as on the first that the aircraft would be there," Dolan said. "We've covered nearly three-quarters of the search area, and since we haven't found the aircraft in those areas, that increases the likelihood that it's in the areas we haven't looked at yet."

Martin was mistaken. Basic statistics will tell you that the further the search vessels moved away from the 7th arc, the lower the probability that they would encounter the wreckage on each successive pass. In the analysis that the DSTG had published the previous fall, it had calculated that there was effectively a zero percent probability that the plane hit the 7th arc north of 34° south longitude or south of 41° south longitude. And the ships had already scanned that segment of the arc out to a distance of 40 nautical miles in either direction.

In September I interviewed the DSTG's Neil Gordon for Popular Mechanics and asked him why his team's calculations hadn't borne out. He told me that the failure of the seabed search meant that one of their initial assumptions must have been wrong. But which one? Gordon's best guess had to do with an event that occured at 18:40, fifteen minutes after the SDU rebooted.

Amid its attempts to find the missing flight, Malaysia Airlines had tried to call MH370 on its satellite telephone. The call went through, but no one answered; it just rang and rang. The nature of the electronic interaction was such that no BTO value had been recorded, so no ping arc could be generated, and the signal wasn't considered one of the seven canonical Inmarsat pings.

But a BFO value had been recorded, and it was telling. Its value was nearly a perfect match with the BFO values of the pings that followed in subsequent hours. Investigators had long interpreted this to mean that the direction of flight had been the same. That is, the plane had already turned south some time before 18:40. This assumption put a northernmost limit on where the plane could have flown.

In essence, the ATSB had staked their entire investigation on this interpretation of the 18:40 BFO value. But what if their assumption was wrong? It turned out that there's another way that that particular BFO value could have been generated. Because the Doppler precompensation algorithm doesn't take vertical motion into account, if the plane had been in a gradual descent—as, for instance, when coming in for landing—then it could have been heading east or north or west.

To be sure, it's hard to imagine why the plane would have been descending; generally when planes fly long distances they gradually climb, not descend. But if the plane hadn't been cruising south at 18:40, then it might have been heading north, or flying in circles in the vicinity of the Andaman Sea, or who knows what.

In any case, a later turn to the south would mean the plane could have crossed the 7th arc as much as 250 nautical miles further north than the DSTG had previously deemed possible.

In November of 2016, with just a sliver of the 46,000-square-mile search area still unscanned, the ATSB convened a meeting of its experts to grapple with all the different ways they could have gone wrong. The results of their discussion were published on December 20 in a report entitled *MH370 – First Principles Review*. The document confirmed what Gordon had told me, that the only way to make sense of the data was to assume that the plane must have wound up north of the previously defined search. The experts defined a new area, 10,000 square miles in size, that straddled the 7th arc between 32.5° and 36° south latitude. Given the signals received by Inmarsat, this was the only place the plane could possibly be. "Based on the analysis to date, completion of this area would exhaust all prospective areas for the presence of MH370," the report affirmed.

On the day that the report came out, the ships were just finishing up their scan of the main search area. At the very end, they ducked into the newly defined area for a few weeks, then called it quits. The search was officially over. To hear the ATSB tell it, their calculations hadn't been wrong; they'd just been unlucky. The plane must have taken a rather unlikely and surprising maneuver and wound up in the newly defined search area. But, due to circumstances out of their control, they would not be able to search there. The failure was not their fault. They could retire from the field with honor.

22.
NOVEMBER 2016

For the relatives of the missing passengers and crew, the end of the search was a devastating development. Back in 2014 the authorities had assured them that they would keep searching until their loved ones were found. Now they were cutting bait. "Stopping at this stage is nothing short of irresponsible," scolded next-of-kin group Voice370.

As I read it, the failure of the seabed search amounted to a repudiation of the ATSB's interpretation of the Inmarsat signals. If the plane had flown south, the seabed searchers should have found the plane's wreckage. The fact that they hadn't meant that Shah couldn't have been the culprit.

But there had long been rumors of a smoking gun, a major piece of evidence that could tie Shah to the act. It had to do with Shah's flight simulator. The captain was such a flying buff that he'd assembled an elaborate rig in his basement, complete with six monitors, two computers, a yoke, and rudder pedals. Back in June, 2014, the Guardian reported that investigators had found computer files on his flight simulator indicating that he "had plotted a flight path to a remote island far into the southern Indian Ocean where the search is now focused." The following January, Byron Bailey wrote in the Australian that he, too, had received similar information, and that "my source ... left me with the impression that the FBI were of the opinion that Zaharie was responsible for the crash."

While these reports were tantalizing, no one had ever presented any documentation to back them up. Then, in November, 2016, Irish journalist Mick Rooney released a portion of a secret Malaysian Police report that included raw data recovered from Shah's home flight simulator. Of 671 save points that had been stored on various hard drives, six were of particular interest. The first four points appear to be snapshots from a continuous flight that takes off from Kuala Lumpur and climbs as it heads to the northwest, with the fourth point located over the Andaman Sea not far from where the real MH370 disappeared from military radar. The last two points are are located more than 3,000 miles away to the southeast. Curiously, at both of these final points the simulated plane's fuel tanks are empty.

Assuming that these save points had been made in the course of a single flight up the Malacca Strait and then down into the Indian Ocean, it looked an awful lot like Shah had indeed practiced a suicide run. I decided to take a closer look. My father-in-law, Bob Masterson, happened to have a copy of the old flight-sim software that Shah had used, as well as a dusty Windows computer capable of running it.

Once I had it set up in my attic I set about running the flight simulator, generating save points, then examining the data files that resulted. With practice I was able to get my files to match Shah's quite closely.

What I found was that rather than a continuous autopilot flight up the Malacca Strait and then down into the southern Indian Ocean, the flight sim user had made a series of disconnected flights, changing his location between runs by manually moving an icon on a map display. In short, what I found didn't look very much like a practice run for a flight to oblivion.

I paid particular attention to the last two save points, at which the plane is out of fuel and located over the remote stretch of the southern Indian Ocean. At the first point the plane is flying at 37,651 feet at close to 198 knots indicated airspeed, which is the speed recommended by the emergency checklist used when a plane has run out of fuel. At the second point, the plane is flying in much the same way, but the altitude had been manually decreased to 4,000 feet. In each case the plane is being held in a gentle descent of the sort one would hold in order to maximize the amount of time in the air.

To me, what this looked like was not a suicidal plunge, but an attempt to hand-fly a dual-engine-failure procedure. Why might Shah want to practice this? Maybe he wanted to see how he would perform in some famous real-life emergencies. On July 23, 1983, an Air Canada 767 en route from Montreal to Edmonton ran out of fuel at 41,000 feet due to an improperly calculated fuel load. In an amazing feat of airmanship, the pilots managed to glide the plane to a safe landing at a disused air base near Gimli, Manitoba. In the aviation world, this legendary feat has been memorialized as the "Gimli Glider."

The parameters of the second save point struck me as strongly reminiscent of "The Miracle on the Hudson," the 2009 incident in which a US Airways A320 hit a flock of geese that destroyed both its engines and then glided to a safe landing in the river.

The overall picture, then, looked ambiguous. Yes, Shah might have been practicing for a suicide flight. But he also might have been trying to become a safer pilot. Bear in mind, too, that he practiced engine-out procedures in a 777, he also flew a historical propeller transport, the DC-3. And three weeks later he played with a Boeing 737. This is hardly the behavior of a man with a monomaniacal obsession with his upcoming demise.

As we've already seen, Shah was a well-liked, balanced, and amiable person. The Royal Malaysian Police folder on Shah also included the results of a psychiatric evaluation which found that Shah had no psychological problems, family stress, money problems, or any other suggestion that he might be suicidal. "Zaharie is an experienced pilot and a competent and respected by peers," the report states. "Information from friends and colleagues Zaharie show that he was a friendly, warm and jokes... we have not found, any changes in terms of psychological, social and behavioral patterns Zaharie Ahmad Shah before his flight."

Certainly, pilots have crashed their planes into the ground and killed all their passengers. But in such cases there is invariably a history of stress and psychological dysfunction. Just a year after MH370 went missing, Germanwings pilot Andreas Lubitz crashed his Airbus into the French Alps. Lubitz had previously been grounded for psychiatric reasons and had torn up doctors' notes excusing him for work on mental health grounds. Shortly before he killed himself, he performed web searches about deliberately crashing a plane.

Shah left behind no such clues. If he did commit mass murder-suicide, he must have been mentally unbalanced enough to contemplate one of the most heinous acts imaginable, and at the same time mentally composed enough to plan it without leaving behind any evidence—not a single Google search, not a single deleted email or stifled outburst—except, possibly, this single set of flight-sim data.

This level of self-control seems psychologically implausible to Katherine Ramsland, a professor of forensic psychology at DeSales University who has written 54 books, including *Inside the Minds of Mass Murderers*. "Usually, there's something that people notice," she says. "It's one thing if you were single, but [Shah] had people around him, coworkers, family. They'd notice something different. He wouldn't necessarily leak his decision or his planning, but there would be something different. To do something like this without anybody noticing anything would be really hard to do."

Ramsland also doubts that Shah would have planned a suicide that involved flying the plane for seven hours after its diversion. "If somebody's going to commit suicide, they'll just go do it," she says. Every other known instance of pilot suicide involves immediately flying the plane into the ground.

Then again, implausible isn't impossible. "There will always be rare instances of things that surprise us," she says. "Human beings are strange creatures."

23.

APRIL 2017

At this point, more than 20 pieces of debris had been found. And for us obsessives who still believed this case could be solved, this debris, more than anything else, was the thing to study.

While Gordon and his team at the DSTG were struggling to figure out where they'd gone wrong, David Griffin's team at the CSIRO was attacking the mystery from another direction. Using data from NOAA's Global Drifter Program, Griffin's team had built a computer simulation of how debris might travel over time. They then ran the simulation many thousands of times to show all the different tracks the flaperon might have taken from various points along the 7th arc. Needless to say, this covered a huge swath of the ocean. Nevertheless, it was possible to calculate the zone from which the simulated flaperons would most likely reach Réunion.

As we've seen, an important component of this kind of modeling is windage. If an object floats high in the water, the wind will tend to push it along faster than if it were deeply immersed. To come up with a windage value for the flaperon, CSIRO scientists built six replicas of similar shape, size, and weight and set them adrift in the ocean off the coast of Tasmania. The results were then fed back into the model.

The outcome was puzzling. Most of the simulation runs ended with the flaperon floating far north of Réunion Island. Perhaps, Griffin's team reasoned, the replicas weren't accurate enough. To explore this possibility, the CSIRO team obtained a real Boeing 777 flaperon, then cut it down to mimic the damage experienced by the piece found on Réunion. When they put it in the water, voilà: Compared to the replicas, the real cut-down flaperon floated much more like the original. Once the new data was fed into the model, it showed that debris starting from within the high-probability search area was more likely to drift to Réunion Island. For the ATSB, this was welcome news. The drift modeling was pointing to the same stretch of ocean as their Inmarsat data analysis.

The CSIRO also used satellite radar altimetry data —super-accurate measurements of the ocean's height over time—to get an even finer-grained look at ocean drift patterns. This analysis narrowed the hotspot of highest probability even further. "The only thing that our recent work changes," Griffin and his coauthors wrote in a paper released in April 2017, "is our confidence in the accuracy of the estimated location."

There were a few problems with this picture, however. One was that, while the CSIRO's refined model was excellent at predicting that the flaperon would turn up at the right place and time, it didn't work so well for some of the other debris items. It couldn't explain, for instance, how a piece of engine cowling had managed to float all the way to the southern tip of South Africa by December, 2015.

As with the flaperon, the CSIRO built a replica of the cowling fragment to test how the piece would have floated. They found that it floated so low in the water that it was virtually unaffected by the wind, and so moved more slowly across the ocean than a high-windage item like the flaperon. When they ran their simulation forward from 35° south, the cowling wound up nowhere near South Africa by the time the real-life object was collected. And some of the modeled low-windage debris washed up on the western coast of Australia where none had in fact been found.

The ATSB's newly designated search zone had another major problem. It lay within their very first search area, and as such had already been partially scanned. In particular, the area around 35° south had been searched out to nearly 20 nautical miles in either direction. If the plane had crossed the 7th arc there and been plummeting near vertically at hundreds of miles per hour, its wreckage should already have been found.

So while the ATSB was making confident public pronouncements, the true situation was much more problematic and baffling. Investigators had developed multiple lines of inquiry into where the plane could have gone, but these lines did not converge. Choose any spot on the 7th arc, and there was a strong reason to believe that the plane hadn't gone there. South of 39.5°S was ruled out because the plane couldn't fly that far. 36°S to 39.5°S was ruled out because it had already been searched. Debris drift modeling ruled out 34°S to 36°S. And a surface search shortly after the plane's disappearance had long ruled out the area north of 34°S.

It was hard to make a plausible case that MH370 had gone anywhere.

PART 3
Capitulation

24.

OCTOBER 2017

It had now been more than three years since MH370 had disappeared, and the investigation was in shambles. The Australian, Chinese, and Malaysian governments had spent more than $150 million and had nothing to show for it. The ATSB continued to insist that the plane must have impacted the southern Indian Ocean near the 7th arc, refusing to acknowledge any of the evidence that undermined that conclusion.

By my own reckoning I was the only professional journalist still regularly working on the story, but I was doing so largely under the radar. Reporters from the mainstream media who parachuted in from time to time were so overwhelmed by the topic that they either simply parroted the ATSB position or fell into the clutches of the numerous conspiracy theorists who constantly circled the topic. It was enormously frustrating and discouraging.

Still, I pressed on, sifting through the evidence and probing for weak spots that might yield a breakthrough. I had accumulated a lot of evidence, but I wasn't sure how reliable all of it was. Some of it, for instance, had come from leaked reports of uncertain providence. And I knew that there were many things the Australians knew that I did not. I kept hoping that they would open the doors to their treasure trove of data. Under international aviation treaties, they were supposed to issue a final report after their investigation concluded.

Finally, three years, six months, and 26 days after the disappearance, the ATSB officially declared its investigation over. In its final report, a 440-page behemoth entitled *The Operational Search for MH370*, it stated that "we share your profound and prolonged grief, and deeply regret that we have not been able to locate the aircraft."

For the next of kin, and for many onlookers around the world, this was a depressing announcement. Personally, though, I saw it as a good thing. For a long time, I'd been frustrated by the ATSB's unwavering optimism, by their insistence in the face of all evidence to the contrary that their efforts were going well. Now, at least, they were admitting they had a problem.

I was also excited to dive into a trove of new evidence relating to many aspects of the case. Particularly interesting was a report in the appendix about the marine organisms found growing on recovered debris. Researchers at Geoscience Australia, a government body devoted to the scientific study of the earth and its oceans, had scrutinized four pieces: the flap fairing found by Liam Lötter in Mozambique, the fragment of horizontal stabilizer with the words "No Step" found by Blaine Alan Gibson in Mozambique, the piece of engine cowling found in Mossel Bay, South Africa, and a section of an interior wall found on Rodrigues Island. The scientists first examined the exteriors of the objects in order to identify any visible marine organisms attached there, then washed the pieces and ran the water through a sieve to collect any small organisms that might have been trapped in the interior or in crevices. What they found had been kept under wraps until now.

Their results ran contrary to official expectations. Given the ATSB's confidence that the plane had crashed in the southern Indian Ocean at the start of the southern autumn near 36° south, the researchers should have found marine life endemic to the temperate zone. But the scientists found no such thing. Instead, every single specimen they were able to identify was native to the tropical zone of the Indian Ocean. "No Step," which had seemed in photographs to be virtually free of biofouling, turned out to have a particularly rich assemblage of marine organisms hidden in its nooks and crannies. "Identified mollusc species," the report noted, "suggest that the item originated from, or picked up, [marine life] from the tropical Indo-Pacific Ocean."

Two-thirds of the species found on this fragment live only close to shore. "The natural habitat of the recovered molluscs is shallow water, on clean coral sand or in seagrass meadows," the investigators reported. "None of them could or would ever attach to drifting debris." The only way the investigators could make sense of this was to assume that it had picked up the shells of these creatures from the sand when it had come ashore.

The age of the organisms was odd, too. The largest of the Lepas barnacles on the Rodrigues item had a shell less than an inch long, which, given the temperature of the water, implied an age of 45 to 50 days. Likewise, the one-third of the molluscs found on "No Step" that plausibly could have attached in the open water were all "juveniles at approximately two months old."

Only two specimens found on "No Step" looked to be older than that. The first was a sea snail of the species *Petaloconchus renisectus*, the second a tube worm of the serpulid family. The former appeared to be six to eight months old; the latter, eight to 12 months old. Strangely, both are usually found living on the seabed. Petaloconchus is only rarely found attached to objects on the ocean surface, and serpulids even less so. "I would never expect to find serpulids on floating debris in the middle of the ocean," said Harry ten Hove, one of the world's leading experts on these animals. "If in the middle of the ocean you would find floating debris with an animal attached, it has to come from anywhere in the world near the coast."

That means that in order to have acquired the tube worm, the item must have crossed quickly across the breadth of the southern Indian Ocean, then lingered in coastal waters near Africa for up to a year—a tough proposition, given that drift modelers already struggled to explain how the object got from the search zone to Mozambique so quickly.

Another appendix of the ATSB report detailed

the work of Patrick De Deckker, a marine biologist at Australia National University in Adelaide. De Deckker had obtained a barnacle shell taken from the flaperon and analyzed its chemical composition in hopes of determining what part of the ocean it had floated from. The shell was 2.5 centimeters long—close, I was pleased to note, to what I'd calculated using my improvised image-analysis technique.

Based on its size, De Deckker wrote, "It could be assumed the specimens analysed here were quite young, perhaps less than one month." This was even younger than what I'd surmised. The brief duration of the specimen's life meant that it had nothing to tell about where the flaperon had entered the water 16 months before its beaching.

Taken together, the evidence revealed in Australia's final report fit poorly with the idea that MH370 crashed into the southern Indian Ocean.

25.

JANUARY 2018

Everyone assumed that the search for MH370 was finished for good. But if we've learned anything about MH370, it's to expect the unexpected. Months after Australia threw in the towel, a previously unknown US-registered company called Ocean Infinity stepped up and offered to restart the search. Remarkably, it offered to carry out the work on its own dime, with the Malaysian government only obligated to pay if the company succeeded in finding the plane.

Malaysia was hesitant at first, but after months of negotiation finally inked a deal in which they would pay Ocean Infinity anywhere from $20 to $70 million depending on how much seabed was searched.

It was a high-stakes gambit for Ocean Infinity. The potential payout was not very large considering that the effort probably cost tens of millions of dollars to mount. Yet if the ATSB's most recent evaluation was correct, the odds would be in their favor. Malaysia's transport minister, Liow Tiong Lai, stated that there was an 85 percent chance that the plane's wreckage would be found within the latest 25,000 square kilometer search zone that the ATSB had demarcated.

Ocean Infinity moved quickly. Its search vessel, the Seabed Constructor, was already steaming across the Indian Ocean when the contract with Malaysia was inked on January 10, 2018. It arrived at the survey area five days later and deployed its high-tech flotilla of eight robot subs to scan the seabed in a grid pattern.

By the beginning of April, Seabed Constructor had searched the entirety of the ATSB's 25,000 square kilometer target area. As I've noted, Australia's stated position at the time was that if the plane was not found in this area, it could offer no rationale for looking anywhere else.

Undaunted, the searchers continued to work their way further up the 7th arc. They reached Broken Ridge, an area of craggy underwater terrain, and zipped right over it, scarcely breaking stride. This feat was a testament to the capability of Ocean Infinity's technology. It also ruled out an idea that had been promoted by certain MH370 theorists, to the effect that the captain abducted the plane and headed for Broken Ridge in the hope that the wreckage would never be found amid the unsearchable peaks and gullies.

But for all its technological prowess, Ocean Infinity found nothing. Week after week the search pressed on. Finally, on May 29, Ocean Infinity pulled the plug. Instead of the promised 25,000 square kilometers, they had scoured more than four times that amount, in an elongated rectangle whose furthest edges stretched more than 500 miles beyond the ATSB's recommended area.

For those who'd labored for years refining their end-point calculations, this final failure was the most demoralizing of all. They'd been so sure they were on the right track. Yet all their meticulous efforts had been for naught. As they mulled over what had gone wrong, they reasoned that there were three possible reasons why the plane hadn't been found.

The first was that the plane had indeed hit the water within the scanned area, but the wreckage had somehow been overlooked. Perhaps it had tumbled into a gulley, or sank into soft seabed mud. Independent Group member Victor Iannello, who had close ties to the official investigation, was skeptical of this explanation. "Sources close to the previous search effort believe [this] is very unlikely," he wrote on his blog, "as there was a thorough review of the sonar data by multiple parties with high levels of experience, and because any 'points of interest' were scanned multiple times to ensure the resolution was adequate to make a determination with a high level of confidence."

The second possibility was that the plane had made its final transmission further north along the 7th arc. But there was no plausible scenario in which the plane could have flown that far, and what's more such an endpoint would be inconsistent with the drift analysis.

The third possibility was that the plane had crossed the 7th arc within the search zone, but had then managed to glide beyond it after fuel exhaustion. This, you'll recall, would be hard to reconcile with the recorded BFO values, which showed a steep and accelerating decent during the final transmissions. Iannello wrote that this would be "possible only if the aircraft first was in a rapid descent (producing the final BFO values), and then the pilot skillfully recovered from the rapid descent and glided some distance away from the 7th arc beyond the width of the subsea search, and then later the aircraft again descended at high speed and impacted the sea (producing the shattered debris). This sequence of dive-glide-dive is considered by many to be a very unlikely sequence of events."

I had long ago called MH370 the triple disappearing airplane because it had successively vanished from secondary radar, then primary radar, and then from Inmarsat. Now, it seemed, the plane had vanished a fourth time.

26.
JULY 2018

Australia had already thrown in the towel. Now that Ocean Infinity had abandoned its seabed scan, it was time for Malaysia to do the same. All that remained of the international effort to find MH370 was a criminal investigation by the research section of France's Air Transport Gendarmerie.

By international aviation treaty, once Malaysia ended its inquiry it was obligated to produce a final report summarizing its findings. And so on July 2, 2018, the Ministry of Transport released its Safety Investigation Report, a document that weighed in at some 1,500 pages. The report contained new information on a huge range of topics, from the mangosteens in the cargo hold to the flotation characteristics of the flaperon. (French investigators still couldn't figure out how an object that floated so high in the water could be completely covered in Lepas barnacles.)

The most interesting revelation was to be found within a report by Boeing that appeared in the appendix. Entitled "Aircraft Performance Analysis," the 8-page document discussed how various combinations of speed, direction, and altitude matched the Inmarsat ping rings. Matching previous analyses, the paper found that the routes that fit best were high, fast, and straight.

Of more novel import, however, was the report's depiction of the plane's path just after it disappeared from military radar.

As you'll recall, MH370 was observed by primary radar as it crossed back over the Malay Peninsula and flew up the middle of the Malacca Strait. It left the radar-coverage zone at 18:22:12. Three minutes later it logged back onto the Inmarsat network and generated the 1st ping arc. It turns out that if you

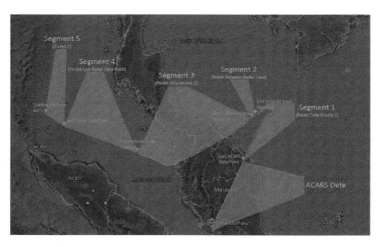

extrapolate the speed and bearing flown before 18:22 and extend it in a straight line for three minutes, you wind up at a point well inside the 1st arc. This means that in order to be on the 1st arc at the moment the

1st ping was transmitted the plane must have turned. Specifically, it must have turned to the right.

A chart on page four of the Boeing report shows this turn. It is a modest one, just 15 degrees. But it is unmistakable. Recall that when the DSTG generated a huge set of routes that matched the BTO data, these fell into two clusters: those that took a slight turn to the right and headed north, and those that took a big turn to the left and headed south.

We now know that as MH370 disappeared from military radar it was turning right and heading north.

27.
CLARITY

To the general-interest media MH370 was a black-hole mystery, a whodunnit of unfathomable dimension. Every few months, the tabloids would run a new, fantastical story: about a satellite image showing a downed plane in the Cambodian jungle; about an amateur mathematician with a home-brew interpretation of the satellite data; about a fisherman who'd seen the plane come down near an island. All these stories added to the fog that had swirled around the case from the beginning.

But for the die-hards who toiled over the technical minutiae of the case the details had grown gradually clearer. It had become evident, first, that someone deliberately took control of the plane and then flew it in an evasive manner until it disappeared from primary radar. But who? A further review of the evidence suggested that there were only two plausible options. Either the captain, Zaharie Ahmad Shah, had taken the plane, or it had been commandeered by hijackers working from outside the cockpit.

Many observers were convinced that Shah had to be the culprit. The recovery of debris from the ocean seemed irrefutable evidence that the plane really had gone south. The discovery of the flight sim data apparently offered an additional layer of proof. But after the seabed search showed that the plane wasn't there, certainty gave way to befuddlement. Two irreconcilable truths stood in opposition to one another. What we had was a paradox.

A state of befuddlement is not what the authorities had promised. From the start of the seabed search officials in charge of the investigation had made a clear implicit promise: we have figured out where the plane went and all that remains for us to do is a brute-force search. We are all but guaranteed to find the wreckage.

As I saw it, their conception of MH370's disappearance fell under the category of normal mystery. That is to say, the outlines of what had happened were understood, so to nail down the details all that was required was a little work. Misplacing your car keys is another kind of normal mystery. You know that you left the keys somewhere in the house, so all you need to do is keep searching until you find them.

The failure of the seabed search, though, suggested that MH370 was not a normal mystery after all but something of quite a different character. Think of a stage magician who puts his assistant in a box, waves a wand, and reopens the box to reveal that it is empty. As an audience member your perplexity goes deeper than simply not knowing where the assistant is. You are unable to make sense of what happened.

Every magic trick depends upon a gap between reality and viewers' expectations. The means by which a magician does this is called the "gimmick." A gimmick might be a hollow coin, an invisible wire, or a misleading gesture.

Somehow, too, in the case of MH370 there existed a gap between reality and expectation. Investigators expected to find the plane on the seabed of the southern ocean; it wasn't there, and they had no good explanation as to why.

Let's take a look at the evidence and see if there's any place where a gap between expectation and reality might have been created. Where was an assumption too hastily made? Where did investigators' attention wander long enough for perpetrators to slip in a sleight of hand?

One feature of the case has always stood out to me: The 18:25 reboot. This was the event that had led directly to the creation of the Inmarsat data. It was the analysis of this data that led investigators to conclude that the plane had gone south. Yet no one has been able to explain where it came from.

If we're looking for a place where investigators lost track of the details, this seems a good place to start. Indeed, there are so many reasons to be suspicious of the 18:25 reboot that I find it helpful to divide them into four categories.

1) It came out of nowhere. Recall that at 18:22:12, MH370 disappeared from Malaysian military radar, heading to the northwest. At that point, the aircraft was completely invisible. The plane could have flown anywhere in the world and no one would have been the wiser. But that's not what happened. Instead, approximately two minutes later, at 18:24:27, someone turned the power back on to the SDU and MH370 reconnected with the Inmarsat network.

In discussing the case, the ATSB has always treated the existence of MH370's Inmarsat data as unremarkable. After all, this kind of data is generated by every plane with a functioning satcom system. But the circumstances here are not normal. There's no reason why an airline captain would have either the means or the motive to turn off this obscure piece of equipment—and there's even less reason why he would then turn it back on again.

There's also no reason why it should have come on at exactly the most fortuitous moment.

Once the reboot happened, the plane found itself in a virtually unprecedented electrical configuration. There is simply no reason why anyone, especially a bandit hightailing it out of Dodge, would want to fly with all the communications gear turned off but the satcom on. Satellite communications expert Gerry Soejatman told me that it is "very uncommon" for aircraft to fly this way. Indeed, out of the ten thousand planes airborne over the surface of the earth at any given moment, not a single one of them is likely to be in this configuration.

Yet because the SDU came back on, and only because it came back on, investigators were gifted with six hours of data telling them that the plane was still in the air. And they treated it as unimpeachable.

2) ***It transmitted an unexpected clue.*** Once the authorities had this data set in hand, it just so happened that it contained a clue as to where the plane had gone. While not quite as implausible as the reboot itself, this too defied the odds.

The Inmarsat data set consists of logged metadata for a satellite communications signal. The system has been carefully designed so that the signal doesn't include information about where and how the plane is traveling—that's what the Doppler precompensation is all about. Yet when Inmarsat's in-house team of scientists examined the data set, they realized that because the system wasn't quite working properly, a residue of navigational information had leaked into the communications signal. It was this residue that allowed them to deduce where the plane had gone.

What's important to understand here is that the vast majority of planes that are flying around at any given moment are not going to be leaking navigation information in this way. For that to happen, a bunch of things have to line up. For one thing, the plane has to be equipped with an SDU manufactured by Thales, rather than the other leading manufacturer, Rockwell Collins. The plane has to be flying under the footprint of a satellite that is past its design lifespan and has run low on the fuel it needs to stay stationary relative to the earth. And the path of the plane has to lie along a north-south axis.

Most planes, as they're flying around, don't meet these criteria and aren't leaking this kind of subtle clue. The fact that MH370 did and was can only be viewed as awfully convenient.

3) It couldn't be cross-checked with any other evidence. To me, even more suspicious than what the evidence revealed was what it didn't. Due to the particularities of the situation in which the plane found itself, there was no other evidence available to confirm the subtle clue encoded in the Inmarsat data.

Because the plane had just flown beyond the edge of the Malaysian air-defense system, and because the flight took place late enough at night that Indonesia had turned off its own military radar system, MH370's presumed turn south could not be confirmed by radar.

Because Malaysia Airlines subscribed to the cheapest Inmarsat service available, Classic Aero, the transmissions between the plane and the satellite did not automatically include the plane's position information.

Because the entirety of the flight track lay under the footprint of a single satellite, its direction of flight could not be confirmed by a log-on with a different satellite. (For instance, if MH370 had flown east at IGARI instead of west, it would have subsequently disconnected from Inmarsat-3 F1 and reconnected with Inmarsat-3 F3 stationed over the Pacific.)

And because the entirety of its flight track to the south was over open ocean, there was no chance for it to be accidentally observed in transit.

4) When evidence later emerged that could have confirmed the turn south, it didn't. The biggest piece of confirmatory evidence should have been the discovery of the wreckage on the seabed. If the data had been valid, the plane should have been found within the search area. The fact that it wasn't should have raised alarms about the data's integrity.

There were other, subtler ways that the Inmarsat data should have been confirmed but wasn't. For one thing, if the reboot had been brought about in the normal way then it should have produced a typical set of signals. Instead, the 18:25 reboot generated an initial BFO value radically different from any of the previous 100 logons, as shown in the diagram below. Investigators are at a loss to explain why this might be the case.

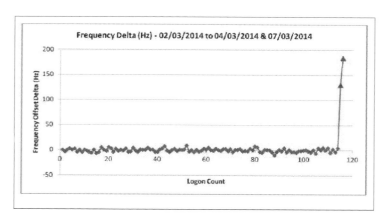

Another problem has to do with the way the debris presumably drifted across the ocean. If the Inmarsat data was correct, then debris should have been collected at times and locations that were consistent with a single drift model. They weren't. And they should have been covered with communities of organisms whose age and makeup reflected their long voyage across the sea. They weren't.

Finally, if the data were legitimate, then the only plausible explanation would be a suicide plot by Zaharie Ahmad Shah. Investigators should have turned up evidence of Shah's suicidality. But they didn't. So we're left with the implausible implication that a man with no manifestations of stress or mental illness spontaneously decided to commit mass murder/suicide. (On top of that, he decided to do it in a way that no other suicidal pilot ever has.)

* * *

One of the most common things I hear people say about MH370 is, "I just can't believe that in this day and age a modern airliner could just vanish." Of course, they're absolutely right. As a rule, things don't just vanish, unless people make them. Magicians make rabbits disappear out of hats, and coins disappear behind kids' ears, and themselves disappear behind clouds of smoke.

If you don't like the idea that something inexplicably miraculous is the handiwork of a magician, then your other option is to imagine that a series of unlikely coincidences occurred. Indeed, every "innocent" explanation that anyone has proposed to explain the vanishing of MH370—like pilot suicide, a lithium battery fire, or accidental depressurization—assumes that the reason the plane was never found is that it experienced an incredible chain of coincidences.

And sure, bad luck happens in life, but once the

odds get truly astronomical it's time to start rethinking your assumptions.

Here's a historical analogy. In May of 1942, the Japanese fleet supporting the invasion of New Guinea was attacked by US aircraft carriers in the Coral Sea and suffered heavy damage. How, just half a year after Pearl Harbor, had America's thinly stretched naval forces managed to intercept the Japanese task force amid the vastness of the Pacific?

There were two possibilities. Either the Americans had gotten extremely lucky or they had managed to break Japan's top-secret naval cipher. The former was a stretch, but the admiralty was certain that the Americans couldn't have broken their code. A mentality later labeled as "Victory Disease" convinced them that they were vastly superior to their enemy. They themselves couldn't have figured out how to break their own most sophisticated code, so they figured that there was no way the Americans could have done it. The Japanese Navy had nothing to fear.

Then bad luck hit again. As the Japanese carriers were moving against Midway Island, lo and behold, the beleaguered American fleet got a jump on them again, sinking all their aircraft carriers. How lucky could those Yanks get? Apparently really lucky, because the Japanese leadership didn't figure out that their codes had been broken until after they'd signed their surrender on the deck of the U.S.S. Missouri.

The search officials tasked with finding MH370 were in the same camp as Japanese wartime leaders. As far as they were concerned, it was inconceivable that they were dealing with an adversary capable of outwitting them. When I asked Mark Dickinson, Inmarsat's vice president of satellite operations, how the company could be certain that the MH370 data hadn't been tampered with to mislead investigators, he dismissed the idea, saying: "Whoever did that would have to have six month's worth of knowledge of what would happen, in essence have to know how the data would be used."

To be fair, some among the Japanese leadership were suspicious of the Americans' good luck all along. And in the case of MH370, some of us have long smelled a rat. In 2018 David Gallo, the Woods Hole oceanographer who led the effort that found Air France AF447 deep in the Atlantic, wrote on Twitter: "I never accepted the satellite data from day one," adding: "I never thought I'd say this....I think there is a good chance that MH370 never came south at all. Let's put it this way, I don't accept the evidence that the plane came south."

When I reached him on the phone, Gallo told me he was flummoxed by the authorities' insistence that the Inmarsat data and its interpretation had to be correct. "This is where I got so frustrated," he said. "The plane's not there, so what the hell? What's going on?"

It now appears that French investigators share Gallo's suspicion. According to Ghyslain Wattrelos, a family member of three MH370 passengers, French investigators are looking into the integrity of the Inmarsat data. "The essential trail is the Inmarsat data," Wattrelos has reported. "Either they are wrong [in their analysis] or they have been hacked."

28.

2ND BATTALION OF THE 53RD ANTI-AIRCRAFT MISSILE BRIGADE

In contrast to investigators' failure to figure out what happened to MH370, attempts to resolve the mystery of the other Malaysia Airlines 777—MH17—progressed steadily. What researchers found in that case provided an eerie counterpoint to my evolving suspicions about MH370.

After MH17 crashed on July 17, 2014, it had quickly become clear that the plane had been shot down by a surface-to-air missile. A 150-pound shrapnel-laced warhead tore open the aluminum airframe, scattering passengers and crew into the 500 mph slipstream.

In most airplane crashes, the question is: what happened? This time, it was: who did it, and why?

The first clue emerged almost immediately, courtesy of Igor Girkin, the GRU colonel whose Reuters profile had taught me the concept of "active reserve." An hour after the shootdown, Girkin had gloated over social media that the rebels had destroyed a Ukrainian military transport. Once it became clear that the plane was in fact a passenger jet, Girkin took down his post.

A consensus instantly gelled among Western experts. Girkin's post meant that the rebels had shot down the plane by accident. Presumably they'd somehow gotten their hands on a captured missile launcher that they didn't properly know how to use and thought they were firing it at an enemy military plane. Virtually every Western journalist, analyst, and government official agreed.

But not everyone. An Internet collective known as Bellingcat started digging deeper. Bellingcat specializes in what its volunteer members call "open source intelligence," gathering information from social media to shed light on geopolitical issues. The loosely affiliated members have none of the academic or government credentials that generally underpin public credibility; the collective's reputation rests on the transparency of their methodology.

Scouring Russian social media, the team gathered photos of the missile launcher that downed the plane as it drove to and from the shoot-down site. In the months that followed, they were able not only to precisely pin down its movements, but also identify where it came from and some of the officers involved in the mission.

They learned that on June 23, 2014, the 2nd Battalion of the 53rd Anti-Aircraft Missile Brigade left its base outside Kursk, Russia, and drove south to the village of Millerovo, near the Ukraine border. Commanded by Lieutenant Dmitry Yuryevich Trunin, the battalion was equipped with a Buk medium-range surface-to-air missile system, including six missile launchers, three missile loaders, a command vehicle, and a Buk Snow Drift radar vehicle. Reaching Millerovo on June 25, the battalion encamped within five miles of an area of Ukraine controlled by separatists, and settled in.

Three weeks later, on the night of July 16, one of the missile launchers, number 332, was hauled across the border and taken down the M4 highway to the rebel-held city of Donetsk. The next morning, it was brought to the village of Snizhne under the direction of GRU officer Sergey Dubinsky, then unloaded in an open field almost directly underneath a busy commercial aviation airway, L980.

Over the next three hours, numerous commercial airliners flew overhead. Then MH17 approached. After Buk missile launcher 332 fired a missile and destroyed the plane, the launcher was filmed rolling back toward the Russian border with one missile missing.

The narrative pieced together by Bellingcat indicated that responsibility lay not with hapless militiamen but with Russia's military chain of command, and ultimately the Kremlin itself. This interpretation was later bolstered by Girkin himself, who in August 2017 gave an interview to the Russian news website *The Insider* in which he was asked who was responsible for the shootdown of the Boeing. Girkin insisted that the militia had not shot down the plane, but also refused to say that Ukraine was responsible. That left only one possibility. "He's implying that Russian soldiers were in the Buk crew, not separatists," says Bellingcat member Aric Toler.

Given the timing of events, Girkin's initial claim of responsibility on social media—which reflected badly on Russia's proxies, and deflected criminal responsibility away from the Kremlin—must have been a deliberate piece of disinformation planned along with the shootdown itself. And Russia didn't just plant that one narrative. It launched a so-called "cluster narrative attack," simultaneously unleashing a deluge of fictitious claims: that a Ukrainian warplane shot down MH17; that the missile had been from a Buk launcher, but a Ukrainian one; that MH17 was actually MH370, repurposed and stuffed with corpses; and so on. To support these claims, Russia generated doctored photographs, released spurious missile-test results, and flooded the internet with chatbots and trolls.

The result was a haze of confusing and contradictory stories. While none of them seemed particularly credible to an informed observer, they crowded the mediascape and created a disorienting sense that all narratives were tainted and suspect— that there was no such thing as truth.

Social media sites like Facebook and Twitter played an obvious role in amplifying such stories, but the mainstream press played along as well. "Western liberal media training proved initially to be no match for the unity of message emanating from Russia. In fact, the opposite was true," writes Keir Giles, director of the Conflict Studies Research Centre. "The emphasis on balance in many Western media ensured that Russian narratives, no matter how patently fraudulent, were repeated to European and American audiences by their own media, and thus validated and reinforced."

These efforts were directed at the world beyond Russia's borders. Domestically, the Kremlin enjoyed uncontested control of the media and so was able to create its own reality.

"The Russian media," writes media critic Vasily Gatov, "have abandoned, sometimes through coercion, but mostly voluntarily and even eagerly, their mission of informing the public and have turned into creators of the Matrix-like artificial reality where imaginary heroes and villains battle tooth and nail in Russia's Armageddon."

In this parallel dimension it was not Russia, but the United States and Ukraine's pro-Western government who were responsible for the shootdown. To the Russian public, the U.S. sanctions that followed were yet another unjustified act of aggression. Their outrage had a twofold benefit for the Kremlin: as with the Chechen war, it united the nation against a common foe (Putin's poll ratings soared), and it provided a palatable explanation for the slumping economy. It's not corruption that's bleeding us dry, it's those nasty foreigners.

Ultimately, the official Western response to the destruction of MH17 was shaped not by the Kremlin's counternarratives but by the assessment of well-informed experts. This was the audience at whom Strelkov's real-time social media revelation was aimed. To these sophisticated onlookers, the apparent gaffe was the found key that fit the lock (remember Teller's dictum). Few of them seemed able to imagine that Russia could be so clever as to plant a narrative that, on the face of it, looked damaging to themselves. It was easier to accept a version in which the underlying cause was bumbling incompetence than one in which the entire West had been taken in by aggressive mendacity.

If the latter were the case, then one would have to entertain the possibility that a nuclear-armed nation with a seat on the UN Security Council deliberately and with premeditation slaughtered nearly 300 foreigners in another nation's airspace for no apparent reason. If one puts events in their proper context, however, the seemingly arbitrary murder of civilians appears neither unprecedented nor inexplicable.

29.

MASKIROVKA

We can get that context by unpacking recent Russian history.

Vladimir Putin was a KGB officer stationed in East Germany when the Berlin Wall fell. Like many patriotic Russians, Putin experienced the collapse of the Soviet Union not as the blossoming of freedom, but as the humiliation of a once-great power. Territory that had once been considered the heartland of the empire split off into independent states. Putin later called it "the greatest geopolitical catastrophe of the century."

Under communism, all wealth belonged to the state, including Russia's vast oil, timber, and mineral reserves. In the brave new world of capitalism, all that was up for grabs. Tremendous fortunes were amassed overnight by people connected and ruthless enough to scoop up what they could. Entrepreneurs with shady connections grew obscenely wealthy while the majority slid into poverty. Birth rates plunged and the life expectancy of the average Russian male fell from 64 in 1990 to 58 in 1994. The nation was literally dying.

A coalition of organized crime, robber barons, and the security forces emerged to hold the society together. In the West, these groups rarely intersect, but in Russia they're a Venn diagram with a lot of overlap. "A mafia state as conceived by an advertising executive," is how journalist Michael Weiss memorably described it.

Putin's rise illustrates the interdependence of these elements. In 1999, Boris Yeltsin, Russia's first democratically elected president, was teetering. He and his coterie of oligarchs had looted the country and amassed great wealth, but there was a danger that once Yeltsin stepped down they would be prosecuted and jailed. To prevent that, Yeltsin selected Putin, then a little-known functionary from St. Petersburg, to be the new head of the FSB, the successor agency to the KGB. Soon after, he anointed Putin as his chosen successor.

When Putin took power, his first official act was a decree that Yeltsin and his family would not be prosecuted.

No one thought Putin would last. He was a political nobody, and headed up a wildly unpopular government that seemed doomed to fall. But in September of 1999 the country was galvanized by a series of deadly bombings that struck four apartment buildings in quick succession, first in Buynaksk, then Moscow and Volgodonsk. Nearly 300 people were killed and more than 1,000 were injured. The government blamed Chechen terrorists, and launched a war of reprisal in which as many as 200,000 civilians were killed. Putin's popularity soared.

The blasts' timing was unlikely the product of good luck on Putin's part. Kremlinologists believe that Russian security forces carried out the apartment bombings as a pretext for a war that would boost Putin's popularity and shift public attention away from government corruption. Among the evidence: undetonated explosives found in the basement of another apartment building that were determined to have been planted by members of the FSB. Arrested by local authorities, the FSB agents were ordered released by Moscow.

Putin ruthlessly consolidated power, jailing oligarchs who failed to toe the line and assassinating journalists who asked too many questions. He was determined to build a strong central idea around which to rally the population, but in the wake of communism's disaster, no abstract ideology would do. Instead, Putin spun together a notion of national Russian-ness that combined a strong central state, patriotism, Orthodox Christianity, and a mythologized vision of Russian history. Putin positioned himself as a combination of tsar and echt-Russian everyman, riding horseback shirtless like a cossack, straddling a motorcycle, and flying an ultralight to guide the migration of endangered Siberian cranes.

Beneath the shiny new veneer of nationalism, the machinery of corruption rumbled along as before. After a spectacular run of growth from 1996 to 2008, the Russian economy stalled in the wake of the worldwide financial crisis.

In 2013, deteriorating conditions in neighboring

Ukraine sparked a full-blown crisis. The country had been led by Viktor Yanukovych, a Kremlin ally. But a people power revolution in February 2014 toppled Yanukovych and replaced him with an interim government that sought closer ties with the West. From the Kremlin's perspective, this represented not a popular yearning for freedom but an act of aggression by the United States and its allies against a country that lay within Russia's proper sphere of influence. It could not be allowed.

Russia had the military might to simply roll its tanks over the border and take control of Ukraine. But it couldn't afford to trigger a world war. Instead, it decided to act undercover by using a military doctrine that Russian forces have been developing since before the Second World War. Called *maskirovka*, it encompasses a broad range of techniques for multiplying the effectiveness of one's forces by deceiving and distracting the enemy.

On February 27, 2014, men wearing military uniforms without insignias or badges seized key government buildings in Crimea, eventually annexing it. The operation was designed to look like an internal uprising, but the troops belonged to elite Russian military units, including the powerful and wide-ranging military intelligence agency known as the GRU.

Inside Russia, the move was wildly popular. Putin's approval ratings skyrocketed. To ordinary Russians, he had stood up to foreign predation and burnished the nation's greatness. Outside Russia, the reaction was outrage and fear. The crisis in Ukraine dominated headlines as Western politicians weighed the imposition of sanctions.

With the deception phase underway, a distraction was needed. Remember when Air France flight 447 disappeared en route from Rio de Janeiro to Paris, in 2009? I believe that Russian intelligence watched that story carefully—and learned that under certain circumstances, it would be possible to make a state-of-the-art airliner appear to vanish into thin air. At the cost of a few hundred civilian lives, you could create a worldwide news sensation, a kind of informational smoke screen to be deployed when you wanted to divert attention from something else.

In early March, international tensions rose as Russia tightened its grip on Crimea. European and American officials issued messages of condemnation. Then, on Thursday, March 6, President Obama took punitive action, signing an executive order imposing sanctions against "individuals and entities responsible for activities undermining democratic processes or institutions in Ukraine."

Russia's foreign minister, Sergey Lavrov, declared that sanctions "would inevitably hit the United States like a boomerang."

The following day, MH370 disappeared.

CNN went to its round-the-clock coverage of the missing plane. Media everywhere turned their attention away from the unrest in Ukraine. Western governments continued to exert diplomatic pressure on Russia to withdraw, but the public was not engaged.

Just about four months later, on Wednesday, July 16, Obama announced new sanctions against Russia. Putin responded with a public statement warning that sanctions "generally have a boomerang effect," and added, "I am certain that this is harmful to the U.S. Administration and American people's long-term strategic national interests." The next day, during a phone call with Obama that had been scheduled the day before at the Russians' request, Putin broke the news of the MH17 shoot-down.

Why did Russia destroy MH17? For many, the lack of an obvious motive made it hard to believe that the Kremlin was responsible. But they were missing the point. "In this kind of warfare," writes U.S. Air Force Brigadier General Alex Grynkewich, "attribution and intent are challenging if not impossible for friendly forces to ascertain."

30.

PASSENGERS

As the official search for MH370 wound down I turned my attention back to the Russians aboard the plane.

Having already probed Brodsky's personal life, I decided to see what I could find about his business dealings. It was interesting to me that his life had turned around after he fell under the tutelage of Vitaly Mashchitsky. Mashchitsky, a wealthy and powerful oligarch with interests in the oil business, is ranked by Forbes magazine the 144th richest person in Russia, But when he and Brodsky first met in the early '90s, Mashchitsky was just getting started, having founded a timber export business called Sibmix.

Among the Russian industries most affected by corruption is the timber trade. According to a 2011 report by Vitaly Nomokonov of the Vladivostok Center for Research on Organized Crime, 80% of the wood in warehouses in the Far East has been harvested illegally.

Could Brodsky be linked to what writer Garrett Graff has called "the Russian octopus—the strange mix of politicians, intelligence officers, oligarchs, criminals, and professionals who surround the Kremlin"?

Looking for clues, I dug into the registration records for his seven companies. I couldn't see any evidence of organized crime links, but did find something else that surprised me. It turned out that between 2007 and 2011, all Brodsky's assets had been liquidated, with the exception of some real estate he owned jointly with four other people. Of particular note was that his main company, "NB," was wound up in 2011, apparently due to bankruptcy. Yet three years later, at the time of Brodsky's disappearance, NB's website indicated that it was processing more than 35,000 cubic meters of timber per year, with an integrated production line that ran from cutting down trees to the assembly of completed homes.

Further evidence that the family was not struggling economically came from business registrations filed by Brodsky's wife, Elena. Between 2004 and 2015 she registered six companies, including a travel agency and several involved in forestry products. The year before NB went bankrupt, she and her two sons founded "NB Company." In 2015, she registered "NB Export." None of her companies has been liquidated.

It looked to me as if in the run-up to his disappearance Brodsky had deliberately wound up all of his business dealings and shifted his assets to Elena.

When I turned my attention to the Ukrainians, I

found similarly unusual dealings. With the help of the Organized Crime and Corruption Reporting Project (OCCRP), a nonprofit that supports investigative reporting around the world, I was able to retrieve business registration documents for Chustrak and Deineka's company, Nika Mebel. On paper, Nika was a failure, reporting small revenues and chronic losses in the years before the men disappeared. Yet when Chustrak and Deineka's families joined a lawsuit against Malaysia Airlines filed by next-of-kin in a Kuala Lumpur court in 2016, their lawyer said that each man had been earning US$2 million a year.

I reached out to Olga Lautman, a researcher who specializes in Russian and Ukrainian organized crime. "It smells like a front company," she told me. "One hundred percent. No one in Ukraine makes $4 million a year off furniture." She added that as Ukraine's main seaport, Odessa is a notorious haven for mob activity. The city's mayor, Gennadiy Trukhanov, has been linked to the international drug and weapons trade, has ties to some of the country's most powerful gangsters, and is under multiple investigations for illegally profiting from the sale of public property.

Deineka's page on the Russian social media site Ok.ru gives the impression that he did have money. In the images he posted there he and his family scuba dive in the Red Sea, dine al fresco in Istanbul, and pose poolside in Egypt. Deineka looks trim, fit, and well-muscled.

I was able to track down a former high school classmate, who told me that Chustrak and Deineka had been best friends at their automotive high school in Odessa. "They weren't particularly good students," he said. "Their interest was chasing girls."

After school both were conscripted into the Soviet Army, as were most of their contemporaries. Deineka served in a tank regiment in Hungary; I've been unable to find out where Chustrak served.

According to court papers filed by Chustrak's wife, the two men had boarded MH370 because they were traveling from a furniture trade show in Kuala Lumpur to a subsequent one in Guangzhou, China. Was that the simple fact of the matter, or was the trip a cover story? The Malaysian International Trade Fair took place from March 4 to 8, 2014, so if they really had gone as legitimate attendees that means they skipped the last day of the show to get to the next one. But the 33rd China International Furniture Fair (CIFF) didn't start until 10 days later. And it seems strange that the men would fly to Beijing to get to Guangzhou, when there are plenty of shorter flights direct from Kuala Lumpur to Guangzhou. Traveling via Beijing means flying past Guanzhou and continuing another 1200 miles, then doubling back. It's like going from New York to Dallas by first flying to Los Angeles.

In photographs Chustrak and Deineka look like they could still hold their own in a brawl. Florence de Changy, who has seen closed-circuit camera footage of the men passing through security, describes them in her book *Le vol MH370 n'a pas disparu* as arriving together, "in the last minutes before the plane boarded, clearly more energetic than their fellow travelers. With their Navy SEAL physiques clad in form-fitting black t-shirts, each carried a big carry-on bag that they tossed on the scanner conveyor belt with practiced ease. Among all the passengers to board this flight, if you had to pick out two hijackers, the Ukrainians would be the only ones to fit the stereotype: age, physical condition, appearance, attitude…"

As of late 2017, two years after Chustrak and Deineka were declared legally dead in Malaysia, they were still listed as the company's owners. Similarly, Deineka remained the legal owner of his family's apartment and the commercial space where his wife runs a beauty salon. His and Chustrak's situation seems to be the reverse of Brodsky's: while Brodsky's holdings were dismantled before his disappearance, Chustrak and Deineka's affairs continue to be conducted in their names. "This is odd," said Ukrainian business lawyer I consulted: usually partnerships of this type are dissolved when the owners die.

Is it possible that Chustrak and Deineka were not really dead, but had successfully hijacked MH370 and taken it to Kazahkstan?

As I researched further I was rather surprised to learn that it is not unknown in Ukraine for intelligence and organized crime figures to fake their deaths. In 2015, a pro-Russian Ukrainian militant named Alexander Mikhailovich Evtody attempted to fake his death after taking part in the artillery shelling of a civilian neighborhood in the Black Sea port of Mariupol.

In October 2018, French police arrested Odessa-based businessman Dmytro Malynovskyi after he forged a death certificate in Ukraine and then holed up in a 12th century castle near Dijon with a small collection of Salvador Dali paintings and a vintage Rolls Royce Phantom.

And the so-called "Don of Odessa," Aleksandr Angert, who made his fortune moving Russian oil through Odessa in the 90s and went on to become a chief patron of the city's mayor, resurfaced nonchalantly in 2019 after being reported deceased in 2017.

Given the questions surrounding Deineka's status, I was intrigued by some of the postings that his daughter, Liza, made on social media. In the year after MH370 vanished, Liza, then 16, frequently visited a site called Sprashivai where users can anonymously ask short questions. Most questions seemed to come from her friends, and asked about typical teenager stuff. Some were about her father, and these she mostly swatted away. But occasionally she gave a different kind of answer.

August 17:
Q: What about your dad (if not secret)? Does he live with you?
A: My dad is temporarily on an unscheduled trip.

September 4:
Q: Forgive the question, but what about your father?
A: Alive, healthy.

Perhaps she was just messing around with her

readers. Perhaps she still clung to the belief that, though she had no particular evidence to that effect, her father must still be alive somewhere. Whatever the case, Sprashivai was not the only website where she referred to her father as being alive. On March 26, 2014, just 11 days after her father and all the other passengers aboard MH370 had effectively been declared dead by the Malaysian prime minister, Liza posted a photo of herself with her father on Instagram with the comment, "Happy Birthday, Daddy." Several friends added comments with their

own well-wishes. "With the birthday boy!" wrote one. "Thank you," Liza replied. Another wrote, "With the birthday boy! Let everything always be good for him," followed by a string of emojis: a blushing, smiling face; a gift wrapped with a bow; a noisemaker; confetti; a toy balloon; a bow. "Thank you," Liza responded, with a kissy-face emoji.

The ebullience struck me as odd, but I wondered

if it might be a cultural thing. For clarification I turned to Olga Lautman, who's part Russian and part Ukrainian, and asked her what she thought. "To put balloons, after someone just died, that's not normal, even in Russian culture," she said.

Understanding that Sergei Deineka's birthday was March 26 helped put another Sprashivai exchange in context. Shortly after midnight on March 26, 2015, someone had asked her: "What are your plans for tomorrow?" She answered: "University, then DR." In Russian, DR is the abbreviation for *den' rozhdeniya*, or birthday. It sounded like she planned to celebrate her father's birthday—an odd thing, it seemed to me, if he'd been presumed dead for over a year.

A followup question came immediately: "Are you going to be together tomorrow?" Liza replied warily: "Watching who you are."

Then, that evening, at 9:25pm, someone broached the subject again: "How was the DR?"

Liza answered: "I do not want to talk about this."

31.

BLAINE ALAN GIBSON

If the hijacking of MH370 was a Russian plot, and MH370 flew to Kazakhstan, then the pieces of debris collected in the western Indian Ocean must have been planted by the Russians in an effort to support the misleading southern narrative. Blaine Alan Gibson had demonstrated an uncanny knack for locating and publicizing this debris. Was Gibson somehow connected to Russia?

Ever since he'd first crossed my radar screen, half a year before he found "No Step," I'd struggled to understand this eccentric character. In the media, he consciously styled himself after Indiana Jones, with a brown fedora and a brown leather jacket. He portrayed himself as an inveterate adventurer and world traveler who before MH370 had pursued any number of quixotic international quests, including an attempt to find the lost ark of the covenant (more shades of Indiana Jones) and an expedition to the site of the Tunguska explosion in Siberia. His was a wonderfully appealing persona. After I wrote about him in *New York* magazine, TV producers started getting in touch with me, hoping I could hook them up with him to pitch reality shows about his life.

I wondered how, exactly, he was able to support such an exotic lifestyle. He described himself as a retired lawyer, based in Seattle, who inherited the money to fund his search after his mother passed away. He said that he'd started watching the MH370 coverage on CNN and gotten obsessed with the case while packing up her belongings. The inheritance must have been a tidy sum for a 60-year-old man, with decades of expenses ahead of him, to have the financial freedom to travel the world full-time. Yet his background did not suggest lavish wealth.

Gibson was born in San Francisco on April 21, 1957. His 69-year-old father, Phil Gibson, had retired after serving as the Chief Justice of the California Supreme Court from 1940 to 1969. The job was well-paying but not extravagantly so; the position today pays $256,059 per year. Blaine grew up an only child. When he was 12, his mother, Victoria, took him on a long overseas trip that sparked a lifelong love of travel.

Gibson finished high school in Carmel and enrolled at the University of Oregon. While working toward a degree in political science he made his first visit to the Soviet Union in 1976, at the age of 19, "just to understand what it was like." After graduating in 1979, he earned a master's degree at The School of Advanced International Studies at Johns Hopkins University. He then worked briefly at a bank before spending three years on the staff of Washington State Senator Ray Moore, who like

Gibson's father was a staunch progressive.

Starting in September, 1986, Gibson took a job with the U.S. State Department. He was stationed in Rio de Janeiro and resigned after one year. He was in Red Square when the Soviet Union ended. According to a profile in Seattle Met magazine, "he could see that the Soviet Union was on the verge of collapse and decided to capitalize on it. For 10 years he lived off and on in the newly capitalist Russia, serving as a consultant to new business owners and fattening a bank account that would later fund his globe-trotting."

When I interviewed him for *New York* magazine, he told me that 20 years before, "when I was living and working in Russia, I was the second American to ever go to the epicenter of the Tunguska meteorite." He explained that "I speak Russian fluently, I have access to Russian scientists, drinking vodka with them, they tell me what they really thought."

Russian is not a language that one picks up on a whim. It is considered one of the most difficult languages for native English speakers to learn. Friends who served in the Peace Corps in Moldova tell me that according to U.S. State Department guidelines it takes three years to become proficient in Romanian but five years to become proficient in Russian.

In 1992, Gibson established a company called Siberia-Pacific Co, domiciled in his Seattle condo, with two co-founders from the Kemerovo Oblast, a coal-mining region of central Russia.

Gibson also registered a company called Russian-American Pen-Pal Service. Gibson dissolved Siberia-

Pacific in 2018, after I started making inquiries. (It's interesting to note that Brodsky, Deineka, Chustrak, and Gibson all made their fortunes by founding companies in the former Soviet Union in the early 1990s, the Wild West era when public assets were being snatched up.)

6. The name and address of each incorporator is:
(Note: A minimum of one (1) incorporator is required.)

Name	Address	City	State	Zip Code
Blaine Alan Gibson	1430 1ˢᵗ Ave. N. suite 5	Seattle	Wa.	98109
Mikhail Piliput	Shishkin St. 25 apt. 69	Prokopyevsk	Russia	653020
Sergei Kuznetsov	Gagarin St. 24 apt. 53	Kiselevsk	Russia	652700

7. These Articles will be effective upon filing, unless an extended date and/or time appears here:

_____, 19 ___
(Note: Extended effective date may not be set at more than 90 days beyond the date the document is stamped "Filed" by the Secretary of State.)

Dated: March 16 , 19 92

Blaine Alan Gibson
(Signature of Incorporator)   (Signature of Incorporator)

Blaine Alan Gibson, Director
(Type or Print Name and Title) INCORPORATOR   (Type or Print Name and Title)

In 1993 Gibson wrote a bill for the Washington State Senate that would establish a trade office in the Russian Far East. In 2002, he took part in a conference held in the western Russian city of Obninsk called "Successes and Difficulties of Small Innovative Firms in Russian Nuclear Cities: Proceedings of a Russian-American Workshop." Gibson gave a talk about navigating the ambiguities between privately and publicly held companies in cities that are home to nuclear power plants, which at that time foreigners were still restricted from visiting. This suggests a deep level of knowledge on Gibson's part about the workings of Russian business.

Glenn Schweitzer, who organized the conference, told me that it was hard to find Americans who had experience doing business in nuclear cities, and so was grateful that he found Gibson. Schweitzer said he couldn't recollect much about Gibson except that he had traveled all over Russia, even to small, obscure places that few Americans ever got to: "I found him to be an interesting guy, because he wasn't like most of the Americans there."

In 2004 Gibson took part in a Department of Commerce conference under the auspices of Siberia-Pacific. The conference was on the subject of "International Travel to the U.S." This time he did not give a talk, however, so it's not clear what his connection to the event was. He was involved in a Tajikistan tourism company between 2005 and 2008, and the company seems to have been active until at least 2013.

Gibson's ties to Russia are more than professional. Several profiles quote Vladimir A. Gololobov, described in an AP article as a "friend" who "met Gibson nearly two decades ago while the American was in Siberia on business trips."

Gololobov was born in 1977 and grew up in Novokuznetsk, a city in Kemerov Oblast. He earned a master's degree in English and German Languages from Russia's Kemerovo State University in 1999, when he was 22 years and Gibson was 42. After he met Gibson, Gololobov moved to the US to pursue a master's degree in International Trade Policy Studies/Commercial Diplomacy from the Monterey Institute of International Studies in California. During that time his listed address was the Gibson family's home in Carmel. In 2002 Gololobov moved to Washington, DC and started working at the Coalition of Service Industries, a lobbying firm, on issues involving Russian trade. That same year Gibson bought a condo in DC that became Gololobov's residence. In 2013 Gibson sold the condo to Gololobov for about $100,000 less than its market value.

When I called Golobov he at first denied that he knew Gibson. "I don't know the person you're talking about," he said, adding: "I haven't talked to the person you're talking about."

Incredulous, I asked: "You're saying that you don't know anything about Blaine Alan Gibson?"

Gololobov hedged. "I haven't talked to him in a long time."

I asked if he'd tell me about how he knew Gibson. He answered, "No."

I reached out to Gibson in hopes he could address the issues I've raised here, but he did not respond to my email.

So: Did Russia plant the MH370 debris found in the western Indian Ocean?

We don't know.

Does the man who found most of the debris have significant ties to Russia?

Yes.

32.
THE PRESENT WAR

Ten days after MH370 disappeared, Vladimir Putin addressed the Russian Federal Assembly. "The USA prefers to follow the rule of the strongest and not by international law," he said. "They are convinced that they have been chosen and they are exceptional, that they are allowed to shape the destiny of the world, that it is only them that can be right. They act as they please. Here and there they use force against sovereign states, set up coalitions in accordance with the principle: who is not with us is against us."

His message was clear. Russia was done playing nice. It no longer wanted to be a complaisant junior member of Washington's club. It had the will, and the means, to assert its rightful place in the world order.

President Obama was having none of it. "Russia is a regional power," he said in response to Putin's speech, "that is threatening some of its immediate neighbors not out of strength but out of weakness."

He might well have been paraphrasing his

predecessor George W. Bush when he responded to the first stirrings of Iraqi resistance by urging the insurgents to "bring it on."

Bring it on Putin did.

In the months and years that followed, the Kremlin unleashed a combination of military force, covert action, hacking, and propaganda that has been dubbed "hybrid warfare." It began by testing its neighbors' airspace with increasing aggression. Its submarines probed their waters. It poured more troops and heavier weapons into eastern Ukraine. It dispatched ground forces and military aircraft to Syria to back wobbling dictator Bashar al-Assad, foiling US plans to usher in a moderate government.

These conventional military maneuvers stopped short of directly engaging the West. In the shadow realm of information warfare, meanwhile, the gloves were off. Teams of hackers launched widespread attacks against Western institutions, probing for weaknesses and exploiting those they found. Armies of bots and trolls promoted conspiracy theories and misinformation in order to disorient the public and exacerbate existing fault lines in society. National Security Advisor HR McMaster has described Russia's efforts as a "sophisticated campaign of subversion and disinformation and propaganda that is going every day in an effort to break apart Europe and that pit political groups against each other... to sow dissension and conspiracy theories."

Few in the West took Russia seriously. The old Cold War bugbear was long forgotten. Now their mental model was the crippled relic of the 1990s: drunk, impoverished, hapless. Mitt Romney was roundly mocked when he described Russia as the "greatest geopolitical threat" facing the United States. Liberal democracy, all right-thinking people believed, had proven its superiority. It had no plausible contenders, as the American political scientist Francis Fukuyama argued in his 1992 book *The End of History*.

That overconfidence opened to door to catastrophic comeuppance. First, a referendum to pull the UK out of the European Union, supported by a Russian disinformation campaign, succeeded in the face of all expectation, setting Britain on a disastrous course to ruin its own economy and to weaken Putin's great rival, the European Union. Months later, intense hacking and social media tampering by Russia helped pull off an even more unexpected result: Donald Trump was elected President of the United States.

Once in power, Trump has moved to validate Putin's critique of American democracy as a hollow shell, laying waste to bedrock institutions through a fusillade of tweets and executive orders. He has attacked the independence of the judiciary, the free press, and Congress. He has inflamed racial tensions and flouted any number of long-standing norms aimed at preventing corruption and nepotism. He has taken a wrecking ball to the world order that the United States forged over the course of the 20th century, trashing America's alliances in Europe, ripping up trade deals and peace treaties, and threatening nuclear war.

The one country that Trump has treated with kid gloves is Russia. He has compared Putin favorably to

Obama, saying he is "really very much of a leader" with "very strong control over a country." He has rejected the intelligence community's assessment that Russia interfered with the 2016 presidential election and obstructed efforts to investigate that interference. And when both houses of Congress passed a law tightening sanctions against Russia with a veto-proof majority, Trump signed it, then neglected to enforce it.

It remains to be seen what the ramifications of the Trump presidency will be. Many who oppose him hope that democratic processes enshrined in the Constitution will eventually be brought to bear. But it may already be too late. Time and again, in places like Venezuela, Turkey, and yes, Russia, we've seen how an autocrat has come to power and gradually subverted the democratic institutions that might have kept a check on his power.

Some may feel that the United States is different, that its traditions are too entrenched, its civic culture too thoroughly steeped in the values of democracy. If Putin's hybrid war has shown us anything, however, it's how thin the veneer of tradition can be. For generations a core principle of the Republican party was opposition to Russia. That antipathy has melted away under Trump. The percentage of Republicans who view Putin positively tripled between 2015 and 2017. In a July 2017 poll, 72 percent of Trump voters said they believed that reports of collusion between the Trump campaign and Russia were "fake news."

"The Russians succeeded, I believe, beyond their wildest expectations," James Clapper, former director of national intelligence, told Politico in October, 2017. "Their first objective in the election was to sow discontent, discord and disruption in our political life, and they have succeeded to a fare-thee-well. They have accelerated, amplified the polarization and the divisiveness in this country, and they've undermined our democratic system... They've been emboldened, and they will continue to do this."

With the United States neutralized, Putin continued his efforts to destabilize the rest of the West. Russian hackers and trolls next targeted the French presidential election, where despite their efforts centrist Emmanuel Macron managed to beat back an unprecedentedly strong showing by far-right candidate Marine Le Pen. Elsewhere across Europe, oligarchs and right-wing populists surged, taking power in Poland, Hungary, Austria, and the Czech Republic. While the American mainstream press struggled to come to grips with the new reality, everything was clearer on Russian-language media. "We are at war with the United States," said member of parliament Andrey Svintsov on state-owned Russia 1. "We may not be using conventional weapons, but we are using intellectual and info weapons."

Do these changes presage an epochal transformation of world politics? In 1814, the Congress of Vienna established the great power balance of the century to come. In 1914, an assassin's bullet in Sarajevo triggered decades of global upheaval that ended with the establishment of the Pax Americana in the mid 20th Century. It may be that the events of 2014 will prove a watershed of equivalent magnitude in the 21st.

If so, MH370 will have a special place in history. The significance is not the plane itself, or the lives that were lost. What MH370 represents is a perfect feat of mastery over the new battlefield: the ability to seize the narrative, to control the enemy's attention so that it can't properly recognize or react to your attacks. In this new age of information warfare, the ultimate victory is one that your opponent doesn't even know has been fought.

Appendix

A SPECULATIVE SCENARIO

March 8, 2014. 12.15am. Kuala Lumpur, Malaysia. A line of passengers shuffles down the aisle to their seats, subdued and sleepy. It's late, and the flight is due to arrive in Beijing at the break of dawn. Most of the passengers are Chinese, with a sizable number of Malaysians and Indonesians and a smattering of Indians, Europeans, Australians, New Zealanders, and Americans. Here, for the next six hours, they will be pressed together in the forced comaraderie of late-capitalistic travel drudgery.

It appears to be an utterly mundane example of a ritual that plays out tens of thousands times a day in airports around the world. But if one were aware of the subtlest psychological ripples that can emanate from subconscious gestures, one's attention would be drawn to three of the passengers in particular.

The first sits in business class, the highest level of service on this flight. A quick-eyed, broad-shouldered man, mid-40s, not tall but physically imposing all the same. He wears a strange half-smile. You can see from his carry-on bag that he is an avid recreational scuba diver, on his way back from a club trip exploring the coral reefs of Southeast Asia. His bag contains a snorkel, flippers, and air-tank hoses. Only if one were preternaturally perceptive would one notice that the bag also contains not one but three full-face diving masks. He settles into a window seat and puts the bag on the empty seat beside him. He unzips a pocket, takes out one of the masks, and stuffs it into the seat pocket in front of him.

Two taller men, about the same age, are coming down the aisle past his seat. Both are well-muscled and carry themselves with the self-confidence of men who prize their physicality. One is shorter and broader; the other has the lanky physique of a basketball player. As they pass the first man's seat, they take no notice of him, but the blond one lifts up the bag with the masks and carries it with him. The quick-eyed man doesn't seem to notice, and neither does anyone else.

It's nearly half past midnight when the doors close. The passengers fasten their seat belts, the flight attendants mime along to the safety video, the plane rolls along the taxiway. If there's a virtue to traveling when most people are already asleep, it's that there are few delays. Right on schedule, the plane lines up on runway 32R, the engines spool up, and the 777-200ER is airborne, heading north and climbing through the equatorial night.

The lights of Kuala Lumpur glitter below, then fall away. Only a few scattered strings of light mark the small cities and towns of the Malayan peninsula, the darker black of the Malacca Strait stretching off to the west. Turning as it climbs, the plane eases to wings level and heads northeast. Throughout the cabin, passengers sprawl in the abandon of sleep, mouths hanging open, heads pressed against window shades or into balled-up pillows. But the quick-eyed man sits upright and alert. Over Taman Negara, Malaysia's largest national park, the plane reaches its assigned cruise altitude, 35,000 feet. Up in the cockpit, the pilot turns off the seatbelt sign and tells the flight attendants that they can begin their beverage service.

The flight attendants move through the business class cabin taking orders. The quick-eyed man politely declines. He waits until they have begun to bring out the food and drink, then pulls his regulator and mask from the seat pocket and moves toward the forward lavatory. Seeing that the galley is clear, he kneels and pulls back a patch of carpet to reveal a hatch with a recessed handle. He opens it, scoots down, and lowers the hatch smoothly above his head. A moment later, a flight attendant comes back to fetch a fresh pot of coffee and sees the carpet askew. *Huh, that's weird*, she thinks, and puts it back.

Down below, the quick-eyed man flips on a light and finds himself inside a compartment lined with metal boxes, flashing lights, indicators. This is the electronics and equipment bay, or E/E bay. Kneeling, he unshoulders his pack with graceful efficiency. He's trained this sequence of moves hundreds of times. With a patch cord the intruder plugs into the plane's Portable Maintenance Access Terminal (PMAT) and begins uploading software. While that's running, he starts pulling circuit breakers and cuts the ARINC cable coming out of the Inertial Reference System (IRS). A hundred feet away, in the rear of the plane, the Honeywell/Thales MCS6000 Satellite Data Unit (SDU) goes dark.

In the cockpit, all seems normal. Starting to feel a little sleepy, the captain rings the head flight attendant and asks for coffee. At twenty past one, the plane approaches the edge of Malaysia's air traffic control zone. Lumpur Radar calls MH370 and informs it that it should switch radio frequencies and call up the controller handling the next zone, Ho Chi Minh. The captain toggles his mic: "Goodnight, Malaysia 370."

Now the plane is in a kind of operational no-man's-land, a limbo between one control area and the next. During the three to five minutes that follow, no one on the ground is paying attention to MH370. And even if they were watching, the plane happens to be occupying an area over the middle of the South China Sea that's far enough from land that surveillance coverage often falters. Standard operating procedure is to assume the plane is where it should be. In the past, that's always been a safe bet. Tonight will be different.

The captain watches on the electronic display as the plane approaches waypoint IGARI, the official crossover point between Malaysian and Vietnamese air traffic control zones. The glowing symbols meet. The autopilot gentle banks the plane to the right, toward waypoint BITOD.

But now, what's this? The captain feels an unexpected sensation. The plane is rolling back the other way, to the left. It's turning the wrong way. Instinctively, the captain glances to the right, to see if the junior pilot has decided to play some kind of wildly inappropriate prank. But the copilot just looks back at him, eyes wide. The control yokes aren't moving, but the plane is unquestionably making a turn.

The captain's never seen anything like it. He's accumulated thousands of hours, done countless runs in training simulators, he even has a recreational flight sim rig set up in his basement, and he's never encountered anything like this. It's as if the plane has a mind of its own. He grabs the yoke. It's like a dead thing in his hands, inert. He feels the tendrils of panic spreading as he grabs a checklist and starts running through it. The more he tries, the more bizarre it gets. Nothing works as it should. Switches are dead, readouts blank, indicators flashing gibberish. Is the flight computer having some kind of a meltdown?

Then: pandemonium. An alarm klaxon sounds. Cabin atmosphere is low and falling. A hull rupture? The sounds of screaming in the cabin filter through the cockpit door. The captain and co-pilot reach for their masks, but no air is flowing. What the hell is going on? Nothing's working. The copilot dials up the emergency frequency, 121.5. Nothing. He punches in the frequency for Lumpur Radio. Nothing. The sat phone is dead, too. All of it. They've been cut off.

The air in the cockpit is noticeably thin. The captain feels like he's sucking air. A desperate idea forms: the E/E bay. Something must be wrong in the

E/E bay. He rises, stumbles, throws open the cockpit door. Two burly men wearing breathing apparatus block the way. He falls to his knees and passes out.

Behind him, the copilot realizes too late what is happening. It all feels surreal, impossible, like a nightmare he can't wake up out of. His vision is swimming. He knows that without oxygen he's got just seconds before he loses consciousness. Frantically, he reaches into his pocket, fishes out his phone, and sends a text, a single four-digit number: 7500. The transponder code for hijack. He's unconscious before he hits the ground.

Now the hijackers are in complete control of the plane.

Because its transponder, radios and satcom have been disabled, the plane cannot be seen by air traffic controllers. But is not entirely invisible. As it completes its 180-degree left hand turn and heads back toward the Malay Peninsula, the plane is within range of both Malaysian and Thai military radar. But it is late at night, and no one has ever launched an aerial attack against either nation.

In the E/E bay, the quick-eyed man still has plenty of work to do. Reaching into his tool kit, he takes out two connectors and attaches them to each end of the severed ARINC cable. Then he removes a small black box from his bag and plugs each of the connectors into it.

He climbs out of the hatch and glances aft at the eerily silent cabin. The thicket of oxygen masks dangling limp and motionless in the half-light remind him of a forest of algae he once swam through under the ice of a frozen lake.

With a shudder he hurries forward to join the other two men in the cockpit. Taking the left-hand seat, he punches a set of coordinates into the Flight Management Computer. They're almost directly over Butterfield Air Force Base, but there's nothing the Malaysian military can do. The plane is rigged to run fast, faster than its normal cruise speed, and even if air force jets stood waiting on high alert they'd have no chance of catching the plane before it left Malaysian airspace.

Just then the quick-eyed man notices a cell phone lying on the floor of the cockpit. It's turned on, trying to put through a text message. The quick-eyed man curses and smashes it. Too late: the phone has connected, briefly, with a cell tower far below. Fortunately, the connection wasn't strong enough for the text to go through. A close call.

The men watch as the symbol of their plane moves across the satnav map. They're heading down the middle of the Strait of Malacca, one of the busiest shipping channels in the world, an ancient nexus between the teeming basin of the Indian Ocean and the great expanse of the Pacific, but at this hour, at this altitude, they are alone. With the wind behind them, they're moving at nearly 600 mph.

The men know they are under radar surveillance; invisible beams of electromagnetic radiation are sweeping over them every few seconds. But part of carrying out an operation like this is understanding not just what your enemies are technically capable of doing, but getting inside their heads, understanding their protocols and their psychology and traditions, in order to anticipate what they will actually do. And they know Malaysia well. Their country supplies its front-line fighter jets. They know exactly what Malaysian military radar operators will be doing on a Friday night. The hijackers know that that their progress across the sky is being recorded, but that no human being is actually paying attention.

That's fine. A recorded performance will suit their present needs just fine. When the investigators begin their search in the light of morning, they will start looking just where the hijackers want them to.

At twenty past two, the plane approaches a navigational waypoint, an invisible marker in the sky called MEKAR. They are 270 miles northwest of Penang, and at the limit of military radar coverage. They have slipped away. With the radios turned off, the transponder silent, and the satcom shut down, there is no way for anyone in the world to know where they are. They have vanished.

The time has come for the genius touch. The quick-eyed man climbs back down into the electronics bay and flips a switch on the black box. It ends its electronic silence and begins streaming position and location information through the ARINC cable to the SDU installed above the ceiling of the cabin near the rear exit. To a human observer, the information would seem like gibberish: a physically impossible combination of values that would have the plane speeding in one direction but winding up in another. But the SDU doesn't care. It slurps up this strange mishmash of numbers and churns out the numerical results that allow it to aim the antenna. It also subtly shifts, by a few parts per billion, the frequency at which it transmits its signals.

A SPECULATIVE SCENARIO

Atop the plane, separated from the cold, 600-mph slipstream by the thin skin of its housing, the high-gain antenna whirs into action, skewing toward satellite Inmarsat-3F1, 26,000 miles above. In a burst of radio-frequency energy, it requests a logon to the Inmarsat system, receives confirmation, and then sits ready. Flight MH370 is once again in contact with the outside world. The thread is as tenuous as one can imagine, but it is there, and days from now, when an Inmarsat engineer thinks to look for it in the company's logs of recorded transmissions, he will be astonished to find that he has the sole clue to the fate of the missing plane.

It will be so subtle, so arcane a hint, that the man and his colleagues will congratulate themselves for their brilliance in finding the clue and discerning its meaning. It will be literally inconceivable to them that another group of men have achieved an even greater stroke of brilliance by planting that clue for them to find.

Five minutes later they are 90 miles past MEKAR. The quick-eyed man enters a new waypoint into the flight management computer. The plane banks to the right, settles into a gentle turn, then levels out again. Ahead lie the Andaman Islands, and beyond them the coast of India and the great delta of the Ganges River.

As they pass over the subcontinent, the pointillistic glow of the cities spreads out below like a galaxy. Ahead, the Himalayas loom like a black hole, the dark emptiness of the Tibetan steppe beyond.

Meanwhile, on the ground, in that great sprawling network of interconnected humanity that is the international air traffic control system, worry is spreading. Failing to find MH370 on his radar scope, a controller near Saigon radios the plane and asks for its status. Hearing nothing, he phones his counterparts at Lumpur Radar. A daisy chain of increasingly concerned telephone calls begins.

At 2:40am, Malaysia Airlines flight operations calls the plane to find out what is going on. A signal is routed through a ground station in Western Australia, up into space, and back down to MH370's satellite data unit. The frequency of the SDU's transmissions will tell Inmarsat engineers who later examine the logs that the plane has turned south and is headed out over the open ocean.

On the ground, the urgency and tempo of the phone calls increase. Meanwhile, in the darkness, the plane that was once flight MH370 is slipping further and further north, high and fast. Hour after hour it recedes from its phantom twin, the imaginary electronic duplicate of itself, which appears to be receding into the vague expanse of the southern Indian Ocean. Hour after hour, Inmarsat's computers check in to verify that the plane is still in range and logged on: 3:41am, 4:41am, 5:41am. The plan, elaborate and complicated as it is, has gone exactly as intended. The quick-eyed man is less than a thousand miles from his destination.

To maximize their fuel economy, the hijackers have programmed the plane to progressively climb higher as the flight progresses. As the journey's end nears they are at 41,000 feet, near the 777's maximum operational altitude.

At 0:11, above the arid expanse of Kazakhstan's

Qizilqum desert, the plane exchanges its final full handshake with the Inmarsat satellite high above. MH370's fuel reserves are very, very low at this point. There are not many places in Kazakhstan that are suitable for landing a stolen 777, and even fewer within immediate range of this spot. There is one, however, that stands out.

Directly ahead, nearly within gliding range, lies a 56-mile-wide oval territory: the Baikonur Cosmodrome, where Yuri Gagarin long ago became the first human being to reach orbit. Though it lies within the borders of Kazakhstan, it is leased by Russia and functions as an autonomous territory—a sort of Kremlin-controlled Guantanamo on the steppe, selected by the USSR at the dawn of the space age for its wide-open spaces and remote location.

Near the center of the oval lies a historically significant airstrip called Yubileyniy, the Russian word for "Jubilee." Nearly 15,000 feet long, it was built in the 70s as the landing site for the Buran space plane, the Soviet Union's answer to the Space Shuttle. Constructed of special reinforced concrete twice as strong as that used in normal runways, and ground to exceptional flatness using special milling machines, Yubileyniy remains the only airstrip in the world built specifically for the use of self-landing aircraft. On November 15, 1988, after a successful three-hour trip in space, the unmanned Buran made its first and only landing at Yubileyniy, missing its landing mark by less than 50 feet. Soon after, the Soviet Union fell apart, and the project was cancelled. Today the area sits largely disused, far from the busy launch areas of

Baikonur, surrounded by derelict buildings that haven't been touched in decades.

Most large runways are located at airports near cities. Yubileyniy isn't. And the fact that it was designed for a self-landing airplane is particularly apt considering that hijackers were chosen for their ability to steal a plane, not to fly it. Fortunately, the Boeing 777 flight management system is able to fly what's known as an Instrument Landing System Category III "autoland" approach. Essentially, once the necessary information is plugged into the system, the plane is able to fly itself to any suitably equipped runway, with or without a trained pilot is at the controls.

As it begins its descent, the plane maintains its current heading, then turns left to line up for a straight-in approach to Yubileniy's runway 24. With the wind on its nose, the plane descends steadily over dry gullies and scrubby pasture. Then it is over the smooth concrete and parallel white bars of the runway's end. The nose rises slightly as the machine settles down onto its landing gear.

It comes to a stop on the reinforced concrete-and-asphalt runway at approximately 6:50am local time, an hour and a quarter before sunrise on March 8, 2014.

ABOUT THE AUTHOR

Jeff Wise is a science journalist specializing in aviation and psychology. He is the author of *Extreme Fear: The Science of Your Mind in Danger*, *The Plane That Wasn't There: Why We Haven't Found MH370*, and *Fatal Descent: Andreas Lubitz and the Crash of Germanwings 9525*, and was an executive producer of the Showtime documentary *Gringo: The Dangerous Life of John McAfee*. A private pilot who flies light aircraft and gliders, he lives outside New York City with his wife, two sons, and a cat.

Made in the USA
Middletown, DE
10 October 2020

21594643R00106